Jewish Holidays and Festivals

Jewish Holidays and Festivals

A Young Person's Guide to the Stories, Practices and Prayers of Jewish Celebrations

DR. ISIDOR MARGOLIS
and RABBI SIDNEY L. MARKOWITZ

ILLUSTRATIONS BY JOHN TEPPICH

Citadel Press
Kensington Publishing Corp.
www.kensingtonbooks.com

CITADEL PRESS BOOKS are published by

Kensington Publishing Corp.
850 Third Avenue
New York, NY 10022

All Kensington titles, imprints, and distributed lines are available at special quantity discounts for bulk purchases for sales promotions, premiums, fund-raising, educational, or institutional use. Special book excerpts or customized printings can also be created to fit specific needs. For details, write or phone the office of the Kensington special sales manager: Kensington Publishing Corp., 850 Third Avenue, New York, NY 10022, attn: Special Sales Department, phone 1-800-221-2647.

Citadel Press and the Citadel Logo are trademarks of Kensington Publishing Corp.

First Kensington printing: September 2002

10 9 8 7 6 5 4 3 2 1

Printed in the United States of America

Cataloging data may be obtained from the Library of Congress

ISBN 0-8065-2429-4

THIS BOOK

IS DEDICATED TO OUR WIVES

EDNA MARGOLIS   AND   RUTH G. MARKOWITZ

WHOSE ENCOURAGEMENT AND SELF-DENIAL

BROUGHT THIS BOOK

TO FRUITION

TABLE OF CONTENTS

INTRODUCTION

The Jewish holidays are the jewels set in the crown of the months of the year. With their brilliance and radiance they cast a glow on the ordinary days and their recurring regularity. They serve as the wayside palaces that welcome the weary Jewish travellers on their mundane voyage across the monotonous, often stark and uphill highways of life. The holidays relax and uplift the Jews amidst physical and intellectual splendor, and imbue them with religious fervor which helps them carry on until they reach the next holiday-palace.

To get the full value of these holidays, it is important to acquaint oneself with their ceremonies, symbols and significance. For this purpose this book has been written.

Jewish Holidays and Festivals

The Sabbath

The first and most important Jewish holiday is the Sabbath, which was given to us on the seventh day of creation. It is also the most frequent holiday, for we celebrate it every Saturday.

Literally, Sabbath means rest. This day is different from the other six days of the week in that it is spent in prayer, religious thought and study in a relaxed and happy atmosphere. The Torah explains that the seventh day is to be a day of rest and cultural growth so that man may be free. If a man has one free day each week, he appreciates freedom and he will remain free at all times. Slaves have no day to call their own.

The Sabbath also reminds us that God created the Universe. As He rested on the seventh day, so does man, His greatest creation, rest on the Sabbath.

Time of Observance

The Sabbath is observed from sundown of the sixth day (Friday), to sundown on the seventh day (Saturday). We begin every Jewish holiday at sundown because the Torah tells us that when God created the world, He considered the evening as the beginning of the day.

Lighting of Sabbath Candles

The Sabbath is welcomed by the lighting of two candles every Friday evening. (In some places one additional candle is lit for each child.) The candles are a symbol of peace, freedom and light which the Sabbath brings to the human soul. They separate the holy seventh day from the six secular days of the week.

The mother, considered by our Sages as the guiding influence of the Jewish family, is privileged to light the candles. She does so also because Eve, the first mother, extinguished the light of eternal life by disobeying God's command not to eat from the tree of knowledge. The present-day mother seeks to repair the wrong done by lighting the candles, and she prays for a long life of happiness and peace.

Kiddush

Kiddush is the blessing recited over wine on the Sabbath and on holidays. The male head of the household chants the kiddush in memory of the first Sabbath of creation and of our deliverance from bondage in Egypt.

Services for Sabbath

Psalms and special poems, *Kabbalath Shabbath* (welcoming the Sabbath), are recited in honor of the Sabbath Queen on Friday evening. *Maariv* (evening prayers) follows. On Saturday morning, *Shacharith* (morning prayers) and *Musaf* (additional prayers) are chanted. Before *Musaf*, a weekly portion of the Torah (Bible) is read. This portion is divided into seven sections. For each section, a man is called to make the blessings over the Torah before and after the reading. The first person called is a *Kohen*, a descendant of Aaron, the brother of Moses and the first high priest. Then a Levite, a descendant of the tribe of Levi, is called. For the remaining sections any Jew can be called. The Kohen and Levite are honored first because they were the spiritual leaders and teachers of the Jews in Egypt and in the Promised Land. *Mincha* (afternoon prayers), the closing service of the Sabbath, is recited before sundown.

THE BEST KNOWN SABBATH PRAYERS AND CHANTS

1. LECHU NERANNENA (Come Let Us Sing) The opening prayer in the Friday evening service. A psalm of the Bible, it is a call to worship God, who created the world and all mankind.

2. LECHA DODI (Come My Beloved) Said on Friday evening; a poem written by Solomon Alkabetz, the Levite, in the 16th century. It welcomes the Sabbath Queen as a bride and declares that the Messiah, from the house of David, will appear in the Holy City of Jerusalem and defeat Israel's enemies.

3. MIZMOR SHIR L'YOM HASHABBATH (A Song for the Sabbath Day) A psalm which praises the justice of the Lord. It was sung in the Temple in Jerusalem on the Sabbath.

4. VESHAMRU (The Jews Shall Observe the Sabbath) A portion from the Torah commanding the Jews to observe the Sabbath.

5. VAYECHULU (And the Heaven and the Earth Were Finished) A portion from the Torah describing how God rested on the seventh day. *Veshamru* and *Vayechulu* are recited every Friday evening.

6. SHALOM ALEICHEM (Peace Be Unto You) When we come

home from the synagogue on Friday night, we chant this famous song welcoming the angels of peace into our homes.

7. (K)EL ADON (Lord of All)   Chanted on Sabbath morning; a hymn describing how God created the planets, earth, sun, moon and stars, and set the laws for their continual function.

8. YISMACH MOSHE (Moses Rejoiced)   We relate how Moses rejoiced when he was given the Torah.

9. B'RICH SHMEI (Blessed Be the Lord's Name)   In this prayer written in Aramaic, we pray to the Lord that we may never have to depend upon Man, but upon God alone. This prayer is said before the open Aron Kodesh (Holy Ark) as we are about to take out the Torah to read the weekly portion.

10. TIKANTAH SHABBATH (Thou Didst Create the Sabbath)   We pray for an opportunity to celebrate the Sabbath in Jerusalem. It is chanted in the Musaf service.

11. YISMECHU (They Shall Rejoice)   The Sabbath observers shall rejoice in the beauty of the Sabbath and find delight in it. It is also recited during the Musaf service.

12. EIN K'ELOKENU (None Is Like Our Lord)   This famous song is very popular with young and old because of its melody and simple repetition of words. It is sung near the end of the Musaf service.

Shalosh Seudoth

Literally, Shalosh Seudoth means "three meals," but it refers to the last and third meal eaten after the Mincha service on the Sabbath. The three meals of Sabbath serve a very important purpose. They strengthen family ties, for the family gathers around the Sabbath table and spends time in eating together, singing songs, and discussing topics of interest. They add festivity and joy to the Sabbath.

Havdalah (Separation)

The ceremony of Havdalah takes place immediately at the close of the Sabbath. A long candle is lit in memory of Adam, the first man, who discovered fire. Blessings are made over wine to remind us of the difference between the Sabbath and the rest of the week, and over spices contained in a special decorative box to symbolize a fragrant week. After the Havdalah, it is customary to greet one another with the words, "A Gute Voch," meaning "A Good Week."

M'laveh Malkah (Farewell to the Queen)

The Sabbath is considered a queen who has come to us to stay for one day, from Friday at sunset until Saturday night. In honor of her visit, we put on our best clothes and serve our best food. When she is ready to depart, we give her a hearty farewell. We eat a good meal, sing Z'miroth (songs) and discuss Torah subjects.

SPECIAL DISHES AND FOODS OF SABBATH

1. GEFILTE FISH symbolizes the mythical great fish called the Leviathan. Tradition has it that this mythical fish is huge enough to feed permanently all the pious souls in Paradise. Gefilte fish, therefore, is a traditional dish eaten on the Sabbath and other holidays.

2. CHALOTH (twisted breads) are placed on the table on Friday evenings, Saturdays and holidays. At the beginning of the meal a blessing is recited over them, and then they are eaten. They are a symbol of the two measures of Manna, the white substance which fell in the desert and was eaten by the Jews for forty years. The Jews gathered a measure each day and a double measure on Friday, so there would be sufficient for the Sabbath, the day of rest. The two Chaloth, therefore, symbolize rest.

3. CHOLENT originated among the Jews of France. It is a combination of a number of dishes (candied potatoes and prunes, barley and lima beans, peas and barley, meat and potatoes), which are cooked overnight and eaten on the Sabbath. The word comes from the French "chaleur" meaning warmth, and from the Hebrew "shelan" meaning "that which stayed overnight".

4. KUGEL is a round pudding prepared for the Sabbath. It comes from the Hebrew "k'agol," meaning "like a circle," or round. It symbolizes a round, good week.

TRANSLATION OF BLESSINGS FOR SABBATH

FOR LIGHTING CANDLES

Blessed are You, Lord our God, King of the Universe, who has made us holy with His commandments and commanded us to kindle the light of Sabbath.

ON WRAPPING ONESELF IN THE TALITH

Blessed are You, Lord our God, King of the Universe, who has made us holy with His commandments and commanded us to wrap ourselves in the fringed garment.

KIDDUSH FOR SABBATH MORNING

And the children of Israel shall keep the Sabbath, to observe the Sabbath throughout their generations, for an everlasting covenant. It is a sign between Me and the children of Israel forever, that in six days the Lord made the heavens and the earth, and on the seventh day He rested, and ceased His work. Therefore, God blessed the seventh day and made it holy.

Blessed are You, Lord our God, King of the Universe, who creates the fruit of the vine.

FOR BREAD

Blessed are You, Lord our God, King of the Universe, who brings forth bread from the earth.

FOR WINE

Blessed are You, Lord our God, King of the Universe, who creates the fruit of the vine.

SABBATH STORIES

Ariel

About 120 years ago, the Jews of Jerusalem were very poor and often went hungry. The Rabbinical Council of Jerusalem decided to do something to stop the suffering of the Jerusalem Jews. It chose one rabbi to travel to other countries to seek help from other Jewish communities. To travel, years ago, meant to spend many days in desolate places, cross deserts full of wild beasts and risk being attacked by bandits lurking in the darkness of the night. Caravans were well armed, and no man dared to risk his life by traveling alone.

The rabbi chosen by the Council arranged for an Arab caravan leader to take him across the big desert. The rabbi agreed to pay an additional sum of money for stopping in the desert on the Sabbath, in order to enable him to observe his day of rest in the proper manner.

The caravan traveled a whole week. However, when Friday evening came, the leader of the caravan insisted on moving on, in spite of his promise to the rabbi. The Arab gave the rabbi two choices: either to go on with the caravan or to be left behind in one of the most dangerous sections of the desert. Without hesitation, the rabbi chose to stay behind in order not to profane the

Sabbath. In vain did his fellow travelers implore him to go on, as staying behind meant certain death. The rabbi refused.

As the last rays of the sun disappeared over the horizon, the rabbi saw the caravan disappear behind a sand dune. He remained all alone in the vast, limitless stretch of sand. When darkness fell and the stars began to appear in the moonlit sky, the rabbi turned in the direction of Jerusalem and chanted the Friday evening service. He then recited the Kiddush over wine, which he had brought with him, and he sat down to eat his Sabbath meal which consisted of bread and water, chanting the Sabbath Zemiroth, as was his custom. He felt there was nothing to fear, for the Lord would protect him.

However, the rabbi was not alone. A ferocious lion was attracted by the rabbi's Zemiroth and chants. As the rabbi turned, he saw the lion in front of him. He nearly fainted with fright, thinking his end was near. To his surprise, however, the lion stretched out on the sand in front of the rabbi, and his eyes shone with peace and contentment. The rabbi lost all his fear, for he understood that the lion was there to protect him. He continued with his Zemiroth and his after-dinner grace until first the lion and then the rabbi fell asleep.

In the morning, when the rabbi awakened, he saw the lion lying on the sand looking at him with great kindness. He washed, put on his Talith, prayed with fervor and gave thanks to his Creator. The lion watched the swaying rabbi, and his half-closed eyes followed the movements of the Talith. After praying, the rabbi ate the second Sabbath meal, sharing his food with the lion. He studied Torah the rest of the day, chanted the Mincha service and ate the Shalosh Seudoth, and in the late afternoon, after sundown, he chanted the Maariv service and the Havdalah.

As soon as he finished chanting the Havdalah, a change came over the lion. He began to run back and forth, and then stretched out before the rabbi, only to jump up again. This he repeated often until the rabbi understood the lion's intentions. The lion was inviting the rabbi to take a ride on his back. The rabbi climbed on to the lion's back, held on to the lion's mane, and the lion and his passenger were off, in the darkness, to a place known only to the lion. They travelled through the night and as the first rays of the sun appeared over the horizon, the lion approached an oasis.

Upon entering the oasis the rabbi found the caravan, which had left him behind in the desert. His fellow travelers were amazed to see the lion kneel and lie down like a camel. No sooner had the rabbi descended from the lion's back, then the lion arose, stretched his full length, roared, and disappeared in the vastness of the desert. The Arab and the travelers realized then that the rabbi was a pious, holy man and they begged his forgiveness.

Since that day, the rabbi became famous as Rabbi Ariel (Ari means Lion, thus Lion of God). A number of his descendants still live in Jerusalem and are respected as pious and learned people.

(FROM *Jewish Folklore*)

The Treasure

It was a hot Friday night in July. Shmerl the woodcutter woke up in the middle of the night covered with perspiration. The air in the one-room hut where he and his whole family lived was so humid that he could barely catch his breath. He got out of bed, washed his face with cold water and went outdoors to cool off.

It was after midnight and there was not a single person around. Shmerl looked up at the sky and seeing the stars twinkle, he felt that only the Lord and he, Shmerl, were awake in the entire world at that moment. Shmerl was no fool, and being an opportunist, he raised his eyes towards heaven and whispered, "Lord of the Universe, now that every one is asleep and You do not have any problems, perhaps You will have time to listen to

me. Please, bless me with one of Your many treasures, and I will
be Your servant forever".

No sooner had Shmerl finished his prayer than a small glistening ball began to swirl and dance in front of him, just like a
Chanukah dreidl. Shmerl was awestruck, but understood that
his prayer had been heard, and his wish was fulfilled. Shmerl
stepped up to the ball, but when he tried to touch it, the ball
rolled away from him. The faster Shmerl moved toward the ball,
the faster the ball rolled away. When Shmerl slowed down, the
ball slowed down too. Strangely enough, the distance between
Shmerl and the ball always remained exactly the same. Shmerl
was puzzled, but he felt that the ball was his treasure, and he
would not let it slip away from him. The ball kept on rolling
and Shmerl kept on following it.

Soon he realized that he had left the town, and was crossing the
fields and meadows, but still the distance between him and the
ball had not changed one bit. Sometimes a hidden voice seemed
to say to him, "Hurry, Shmerl, and throw your robe over the
treasure, and then it will be yours." Shmerl realized that this
could only be the voice of Satan who wanted him to commit a sin
on the Sabbath. For to pick up the treasure and carry it home
would create a commotion there. His wife would tell the neighbors, the whole town would gather in front of his home instead
of attending services in the Shul, and that would cause Jews to
profane the Sabbath. Shmerl slowed his pace; no one would make
him profane the Sabbath and be a bad example to others. The
ball also slowed its pace.

While following the rolling treasure Shmerl thought: "If I
could only get hold of the treasure without profaning the Sabbath,
it would be so good. In my old age, I would not have to work so
hard any more, and I would buy fine clothes for my faithful
wife, who has worked so hard all her life and cannot afford a new
dress. I would give my children the best education possible, so
they would not have to be ignorant, as I am. I would buy a house

with three rooms and not have to live in a one-room hut, especially during the hot summer days. Maybe it would not be such a great sin to grab the treasure now, and then give charity to atone for this little sin. Of course, I would do it only for the sake of my wife and my poor children, but . . . these are only Satanic thoughts. If I am worthy of the treasure, I'll get it the right way!"

Shmerl raised his eyes to heaven and said: "Master of the World, whom are you teasing? Are you teasing me, Shmerl the woodcutter? If you want to give me a treasure, please give it to me, but don't play tricks on me."

Suddenly, Shmerl noticed that he was already approaching the next village. He had walked a long distance, and in anger, he turned back towards his home.

"I will not follow you any more," he said to the ball. "The Lord does not make fun of people. Satan must have overheard my prayer and has been trying to tease me."

As he turned back, the glistening ball jumped ahead of him and again began to roll back toward his home town, keeping the same distance as before.

"I won't tell anybody about this incident," Shmerl thought. "Most people won't believe me, and some will laugh at me. I won't even tell my wife. She may get angry with me and call me Shlumiel, Good-for-nothing." I had one good chance in my lifetime and missed it. My Creator and I know about it, and that is enough for me. Anyhow, why should I get excited about a treasure? What is money? Nothing. It is just an instrument of sin, murder and cheating. I am better off without the treasure."

Shmerl was approaching his hut. The door was still open as he had left it. The ball rolled ahead of him through the door, into the hut, and right under the bed. Shmerl took his robe and threw it over the swirling ball. Quietly he got into bed, but could not sleep. And again he resolved not to tell anybody about his experience until after sundown.

Because Shmerl showed strength of character and did not profane the Sabbath, the treasure remained under his bed. He found it after he had chanted the Havdalah, but instead of the ball, he found a sack full of gold. Shmerl became the richest man in town. Yet his wife complained from time to time.

"What kind of a man did I marry, a man with a heart of stone? A whole day long he hid a treasure under his bed without uttering a word, without betraying his emotions to me, his devoted wife. And maybe," she added with a hurt look, "the treasure did not disappear during the day because of my prayers mixed with tears, and not because of my stone-hearted husband's particular virtues."

Shmerl, feeling guilty, tried to pacify her: "I am sure that only your prayers kept the treasure in place. I only brought it to your home." And then they would look at each other, and the smiles on their faces would show the deep love and devotion they felt.

(I. L. PERETZ)

SABBATH QUESTIONS

True or False

Sabbath means rest.
Sabbath or any holiday is observed from sundown to sundown.
Musaf comes before Shacharith.
L'cha Dodi is chanted at Mincha service.
Three men are called to the Torah on Sabbath.
M'lave Malka is a prayer.
Shalosh Seudoth is a holiday.
Havdalah is performed on Saturday night.
Kiddush is recited on Friday evening.

Draw a Line Under the Correct Answer

Yom Tov is: a good day, a fast day, a rainy day.
Sabbath begins at sundown, morning, midnight.
Kiddush is a chant over wine, a prayer for the dead, blessing over
  herbs.
Kohen is a priest, prince, cantor.
Mincha is a service in the afternoon, morning, evening.
Maariv is a service, in the afternoon, morning, evening.
Shacharith is a service in the afternoon, morning, evening.
Musaf is a service in the afternoon, morning, evening.
Shalom Aleichem is a chant, the name of a writer, a Hebrew
  greeting.

Why

Why do we observe Sabbath every seventh day?
Why do we light candles?
Why do we make Kiddush?
Why do we use Chaloth?

Why do we read a portion of the Torah and Prophets each Sabbath?

Why do we make Havdalah?

When

When do we observe the Sabbath?

Light candles?

Chant Kiddush?

Chant Kabbalath Shabbath?

Observe Shalosh Seudoth?

Eat Cholent, Kugel, Gefilte fish?

Who Are the Following

A rabbi, a gabbai, a chazan, a baal koreh, kohen, levi, Israelite?

General Questions

How do you observe the Sabbath?

Why do you think that Sabbath is so important to Jewish life?

Do you like the observance of Sabbath and why?

How do you connect Israel with the Sabbath?

How do you participate in Sabbath services?

How do you make Sabbath enjoyable and pleasant?

What does Sabbath mean literally and spiritually?

Rosh Hashanah

(THE JEWISH NEW YEAR)

Rosh Hashanah means the head or beginning of the Jewish year. It is the birthday of the world, for tradition tells us that the world was created then.

Rosh Hashanah is the day when God judges each man according to his deeds—good and bad. It is therefore also known as "Yom Hazikaron," the Day of Remembrance, and "Yom Hadin," the Day of Judgment.

Rosh Hashanah is also known as "Yom Teruah," the day of the blowing of the Shofar (ram's horn), which is blown to remind us to repent for our sins, because this is the day of judgment. The use of the Shofar goes back to the time of our ancestors when Abraham was willing to sacrifice his only son Isaac, when God told him to do so, in order to test Abraham. At the last moment, the Almighty commanded Abraham to substitute the ram for Isaac. By blowing the horn, we seek to recall Abraham's complete faith in the Lord.

Time of Observance

Rosh Hashanah is observed for two days. It comes on the first and second days of the Hebrew month of Tishri (usually in September), which is the first month of the Hebrew calendar. Like the Sabbath, it begins on the evening before the first day, with the lighting of candles, and ends at nightfall of the second day.

Rosh Hashanah Greetings

On Rosh Hashanah, as judgment day, the decision of the Lord concerning the lot of each Jew is noted in special symbolic books. Every righteous Jew has his name entered in the Book of Life immediately. Therefore, upon leaving the synagogue after the Maariv service, on the eve of Rosh Hashanah, as well as on meeting a friend on either day of the holiday, the greeting is, "L'Shanah Tova Tikasevu," which means, "May you be inscribed in the Book of Life for the next year."

Selichoth

The High Holy Days begin with the special services known as *Selichoth*, prayers asking forgiveness (from the Hebrew "Slicha" meaning forgiveness). These *Selichoth* are usually chanted after midnight, beginning a week before Rosh Hashanah, and continuing to Yom Kippur. They are said after midnight to show our sincerity and our readiness to sacrifice sleep for forgiveness.

The Ten Days of Repentance

The ten days beginning with the first day of Rosh Hashanah and ending with Yom Kippur, are called the "Ten Days of Repentance." During these days, we regret our sins, ask God's forgiveness, and resolve to mend our ways during the coming year.

Fast of Gedaliah

After the destruction of the First Jewish Temple in Jerusalem, Nebuchadnezzar, the conquering king of Babylon, appointed a Jewish governor for Judea. This governor was called Gedaliah. As long as Gedaliah was governor, the Jews hoped that they would soon regain their rights and their independence. Unfortunately, the Egyptians conspired to have Gedaliah murdered. The Jews in Jerusalem then fled, and with them went, for a long time, the Jewish cultural center in Israel. The whole course of Jewish history might well have been different had Gedaliah lived. In remembrance of the death of Gedaliah, a fast day is observed on the day following Rosh Hashanah, or the third day of Tishri.

THE BEST KNOWN ROSH HASHANAH PRAYERS

Since Rosh Hashanah is the day of judgment, the prayers stress the greatness and everlastingness of the Lord who is the Judge.

1. ZOCHREINU L'CHAIM (Remember Us to Life) A prayer said at each of the seven services of Rosh Hashanah, requesting the Lord to remember us and inscribe us in the Book of Life.
2. HASHEM MELECH (The Lord Is King) This prayer, said at the morning and Musaf services on Rosh Hashanah, declares that the Lord is, was, and will be, King of the universe.
3. L'EL ORECH DIN (To the Lord Who Sits in Judgment) A prayer arranged alphabetically, which describes the way the Lord judges mankind on Rosh Hashanah.

4. AVINU MALKENU (Our Father, Our King) This prayer lists many requests that we ask of the Lord for the New Year.

5. UNESANEH TOKEF (Let Us Tell How Holy Is This Day) This prayer said both days of Rosh Hashanah at the morning service, describes how all get ready for judgment on Rosh Hashanah, and how the Lord decides what shall be each one's fate during the coming year.

6. VECHOL MAAMINIM (Everyone Believes) This prayer describes God's power, kindness, and readiness to forgive.

The Torah Readings on Rosh Hashanah

On each of the two days of Rosh Hashanah, portions of the Bible are read between Shacharith (morning prayer) and Musaf. On the first day, that part of the Book B'reshith is read which tells of the birth of Isaac, and of Ishmael's leaving Abraham's house. The reading from the Early Prophets describes the birth of Samuel and his training for prophecy in the home of the High Priest Eli.

The reading from the Torah on the second day of Rosh Hashanah tells about the readiness of Abraham to sacrifice his only son, Isaac, when the Lord, in order to test him, orders him to do so. At the last moment, Abraham is told to sacrifice a ram instead of Isaac.

SPECIAL ROSH HASHANAH CUSTOMS

TASHLICH In the afternoon of Rosh Hashanah, prayers are said at a river or any other body of running water. There we symbolically throw away our sins which are carried off by the running water.

SPECIAL FOODS We eat round Challah, honey, and new fruits, to symbolize the hope that the coming year will be round, smooth and sweet. We say a special blessing, "Shehecheyanu," to thank God for keeping us alive this far.

We also eat *Tzimes* which is a dish made from carrots. The Yiddish word for carrots is "Meyrin" which means to increase. Therefore, we eat Tzimes on Rosh Hashanah as a symbol that God will increase our privileges.

TRANSLATION OF BLESSINGS FOR ROSH HASHANAH

FOR LIGHTING CANDLES

Blessed are You, Lord our God, King of the Universe, who sanctified us with His commandments and commanded us to light the candle of the festival.

Blessed are You, Lord our God, King of the Universe, who has kept us alive and preserved us, and enabled us to reach this present time.

ROSH HASHANAH GREETING

You shall be inscribed in the Book of Life for a happy year.

FOR A NEW FRUIT

Blessed are You, Lord our God, King of the Universe, creator of the fruit of the tree.

Blessed are You, Lord our God, King of the Universe, who has kept us alive and preserved us, and enabled us to reach this present time.

FOR HONEY

May it be the will of God to grant us a sweet and good New Year.

FOR WINE

Blessed are You, Lord our God, King of the Universe, creator of the fruit of the vine.

FOR TALITH

Blessed are You, Lord our God, King of the Universe, who has sanctified us with his commandments, and commanded us to wrap ourselves in the fringed garment.

ROSH HASHANAH FOLKLORE

Rabbi Amnon

In the city of Mayence, there lived a famous rabbi by the name of Rabbi Amnon whom the King respected and liked. But the King had an advisor who was jealous of Rabbi Amnon and tried to get rid of him. He kept on telling the King that he should force Rabbi Amnon to become a Christian.

One day, the King weakened and ordered Rabbi Amnon to accept Christianity. Rabbi Amnon asked for three days to think it over. The King granted Rabbi Amnon's request, thinking that the rabbi would then accept Christianity.

After the three days passed, Rabbi Amnon refused to come to the King, because he knew what awaited him when he refused to accept Christianity. The King was very angry that the rabbi had disobeyed him, and he ordered Rabbi Amnon to be brought before him. The King asked, "Why did you not come to give me the answer after three days?" Rabbi Amnon answered, "Because I did not want to accept Christianity." The King said, "Because you have refused to obey the order, you shall be severely punished. Your feet, which refused to carry you, shall be cut off." The guards obeyed the King's command. It happened to be Rosh Hashanah, and the bleeding rabbi asked to be brought to the synagogue. He asked to be permitted to say a prayer. Then he composed and recited the famous prayer, "Unesaneh Tokef," and when he had finished it, he died in the synagogue.

In honor of the martyred rabbi, and because the prayer describes how the Lord judges everyone on the High Holy Days, it is the custom to chant this prayer on Rosh Hashanah and on Yom Kippur in every synagogue and temple all over the world.

The Tzadik of Nemirov

Every year during Selichoth time, the Tzadik (Holy Rabbi) of Nemirov disappeared. His family came to Shul during the midnight service of Selichoth, but the Tzadik could not be found either in the Shul or at his home. He simply disappeared.

When non-believers chided the rabbi's followers concerning his disappearance, his followers insisted that the rabbi went to heaven to defend and plead for poor Jews accused by Satan of doing wrong. In heaven, the rabbi was able to challenge Satan directly before the Master of the world, they said.

Once a Jew, not a follower of the Tzadik, visited the synagogue on Selichoth night. Upon being told about the disappearance of the rabbi, he decided to investigate the whole thing.

The Jew stole into the rabbi's bedroom and hid himself under the rabbi's bed. When midnight came, he heard the family get up, dress and leave for the synagogue. The rabbi did not move. When silence reigned in his home, the rabbi, moaning and groaning, got up from his bed, and to the Jew's consternation, dressed in the clothes of a Russian peasant, smeared his face with soot so as not to be recognized, took a heavy ax and left the house. The Jew followed with a question in his mind: "He may be a rabbi in the day time and a bandit during the night."

The rabbi walked in the shadows of the houses so as not to be seen, until he had left the town and entered a forest. The Jew was very frightened, but his curiosity got the best of him and he followed the rabbi deep into the forest. At one place, the rabbi stopped, took his ax and cut down a tree. He then chopped it into smaller pieces, tied them in a bundle, and went on. He finally came to a clearing in the forest. The Jew saw the rabbi approach a small hut in the clearance, and knock at the door. A woman's weak voice asked. "Who is there?"

"This is Vasil, the peasant," the rabbi answered in Russian.

"What do you want, Vasil?"

"I brought you some wood because you are sick."

"But how much will it cost me?"

"Six kopecks."

"But I do not have the money, nor do I know when I will have it."

The rabbi got angry. In a gruff and scolding voice, he said to her, "I, a plain Russian peasant, am willing to trust you with six kopecks, but you, who have such a great Lord in heaven, do not want to trust in Him for six kopecks. You ought to be ashamed of yourself."

Slowly, a weak hand opened the door and let the rabbi in. The Jew ran to the window and looked inside. He saw the rabbi light the stove, and then heat some water, make tea, and give it to the woman, who was sick and cold. While doing this, he chanted the Selichoth in a low voice. . . .

The Jew thereafter became one of the staunchest supporters and followers of the Rabbi. Upon hearing people tell about the Tzadik of Nemirov going to heaven to intercede for the poor people, he would add:

"Who knows?"—if not even higher than that."

(I. L. PERETZ)

ROSH HASHANAH QUESTIONS

True or False

Rosh Hashanah means the holiday of fruit.

Rosh Hashanah is observed on the first and second days of Tishri.

Tashlich is a ceremony of symbolically throwing away our sins.

The Ten Days of Repentance begin with Rosh Hashanah and end with Yom Kippur.

Selichoth are books.

Shehecheyanu is a blessing.

Fast of Gedaliah is observed on Rosh Hashanah.

L'Shanah Tova Tikasevu means: "May you be inscribed in the Book of Life for the next year."

Draw a Line Under the Correct Answer

Rosh Hashanah means: head of the tribe, head of the year, head of the month.

Selichoth are: branches of trees, prayers, books.

Tashlich means: ceremony over wine, casting sins in water, thanksgiving.

Shehechyanu is: A blessing of thanksgiving, for fruit, for bread.

Gedaliah was killed because: the Jews did not like him, the Egyptians did not like him, the Babylonians did not like him.

A Machzor is: a holiday prayer book, a daily prayer book, a science book.

Why

Why do we blow the Shofar on Rosh Hashanah?

Eat a round Challah?

Chant the blessing Shehecheyanu?

Eat honey?

Call Rosh Hashanah: Yom Hazikaron, Yom Hadin, Yom Teruah?

General Questions

What kind of a calendar do we Jews use?

Could you mention the names of the months in the Jewish calendar?

Why is Rosh Hashanah observed on the first two days of Tishri?

Why should a Jew observe Rosh Hashanah?

How do you observe Rosh Hashanah?

How could Rosh Hashanah observance help you in your future life?

Do you make it a practice to greet every person every day?

Do you make it a practice to greet people with L'Shanah Tovah on Rosh Hashanah?

Why are greetings so important in everyone's life?

Yom Kippur

Yom Kippur (The Day of Forgiveness or Atonement) comes on the tenth day of the Jewish month of Tishri (September or October). It is the last of the Ten Days of Repentance, and is the most solemn day of the Jewish calendar. It is believed that those who have not been good enough to be written into the Book of Life immediately on Rosh Hashanah, are given ten days to repent, pray for forgiveness, and do good deeds until Yom Kippur, when their fate will be decided. The entire day of Forgiveness (Yom Kippur) is spent in fasting and praying.

Time of Observance

Yom Kippur is observed from before sundown on the ninth day of the Hebrew month of Tishri to sundown on the tenth day of the Hebrew month of Tishri. The supper meal is eaten before sundown. Then the mother lights the candles with a special blessing for Yom Kippur. The father blesses mother and each child before going to the synagogue.

Services for Yom Kippur

The opening service of Yom Kippur evening is the traditional Kol Nidre which is followed by the Maariv service. The next morning, the Shacharith Service is said, followed by the reading of the Torah portion. Then the Musaf service is chanted. Late in the afternoon, the Mincha service is said, followed by the closing Yom Kippur service called Neilah. At the end of Neilah, the Shofar is blown to signify the end of Yom Kippur.

THE BEST KNOWN YOM KIPPUR PRAYERS

1. KOL NIDRE (All Vows) is recited before sundown on the eve of Yom Kippur. The cantor chants this prayer while surrounded by the elders of the congregation, who hold Torah scrolls. Kol Nidre is a declaration that all promises made by man to God and to himself during the next year, which he will not be able to keep, shall be null and void. However, vows and promises made by anyone to his fellow man are not cancelled by the Kol Nidre declaration.

2. SHEMA KOLENU (Hear Our Cry) This prayer is recited toward the end of each service on Yom Kippur. In it we ask the Lord to have mercy on us, accept our prayers and always be with us.

3. AL CHET (For the Sin) This prayer also is recited toward the end of each service on Yom Kippur. In it we list the sins for which we ask the Lord's forgiveness.

4. ALENU LESHABEACH (It Is Our Duty to Praise) This prayer which concludes the three daily services throughout the year has a special place in the Musaf service of Yom Kippur. When

the cantor repeats aloud this prayer he kneels to the floor when he proclaims the Lord as the King of Kings, the Holy One Blessed Be He. He is then helped to his feet to continue the service.

5. KEE ANU AMECHA (For We Are Your People)   This too is repeated in every one of the services of Yom Kippur. We ask the Lord to forgive our sins because we are His people and children and He is our God and Father.

6. NEILAH (Closing)   This is the closing or final service of Yom Kippur. It is the Jewish belief that the gates of heaven are open during the Days of Repentance to receive our prayers for forgiveness and that they close after the Neilah service. The Neilah service is very beautiful, and the Jews stand throughout the service. They pray that the good lot which they hope has been assigned to them earlier, should receive the final seal of approval at the Neilah service.

Torah Readings for Yom Kippur

The Torah is read twice on Yom Kippur day, once after the Shacharith service and again at the Mincha service. In the morning we read that portion of the book of Leviticus which describes the service conducted by the High Priest in the Temple on Yom Kippur.

At the Mincha service we read the portion of Leviticus which tells us which relatives one can or cannot marry. This portion cautions us not to do the immoral things that the former inhabitants of the Land of Israel did, if we wish to remain in the land. We also read about the prophet Jonah, who was sent to tell Nineveh, the wicked city of Assyria, that it was to be destroyed because it was full of sin. Jonah ran away on a boat in order not to preach to Nineveh. A storm arose and he was thrown overboard by his fellow travellers, when they found out that he was running away from the Lord. A whale swallowed him and brought him back. Jonah then realized that there is no escape from God and he did as he was told. This is read on Yom Kippur in order to bring home to the Jews that God is everywhere.

YOM KIPPUR FOLKLORE

Rabbi Salanter and Kol Nidre

Once there was a great rabbi by the name of Rabbi Israel Salanter. On one Yom Kippur eve, when the whole congregation was waiting in the synagogue for their rabbi to chant the Kol Nidre, as they would not start the service without him, the rabbi did not arrive. They waited and waited and finally sent a messenger to the rabbi's house, but the rabbi was not home either. They could not understand where the rabbi had disappeared. Finally, after two hours of waiting and searching for the rabbi, they saw him entering the synagogue. When asked for an explanation, the much revered rabbi explained, "When I was walking to the synagogue this evening, I passed a house where a little child was crying. It seems that the mother went to the synagogue and left the child sleeping. So I went into the house and took care of the baby until he fell asleep, as I believe that a crying baby is more important than the chanting of Kol Nidre on time."

The Tzadik

During the Neilah, or closing, service of Yom Kippur, a great Hasidic Rabbi was standing in the pulpit, chanting the prayers in his role of Shliach Tzibur, or messenger of the congregation, since who was worthier than he of being the Shliach Tzibur? Suddenly, the rabbi stopped chanting as if he were paralyzed— his body shook but not a sound came from his throat. The people were puzzled. Minutes passed by, half an hour passed, an hour passed, and still there was no sound. It was late in the day and the people in the synagague were anxious to go home to break their fast, but they did not move from their seats, and complete silence reigned in the synagogue. The adherents of the holy man suspected that the rabbi was in communication with God and, therefore, must not be disturbed.

In the meantime, Yosel, the eight-year-old son of a farmer who had come to the village to pray, came to the synagogue to wait for Yom Kippur to come to an end and walk home with his father. As Yosel arrived at the entrance of the synagogue, he was overwhelmed by the complete silence. He saw all the people standing silently and staring at the great rabbi. Yosel stood awed by the sight, and quite suddenly, he felt like praying to God. The urge to pray became stronger and stronger by the minute; he *must* express himself. Since Yosel lived on a farm and had not been given the opportunity of learning the prayers in Hebrew, the only way he knew of expressing his joys and sorrows was by whistling.

Suddenly, the entire congregation heard a piercing whistle at the door of the synagogue. Many hurried to find the culprit who had dared do such a thing while the rabbi was in communication with God. But the holy man, as if coming to life suddenly, asked, "Where is the great Tzadik who whistled from the depths of his heart and pierced the gates of heaven, and thus caused God to nullify the severe decree?" But the Tzadik could not be found anywhere.

(J. L. PERETZ)

YOM KIPPUR QUESTIONS

True or False

Yom Kippur is the Day of Atonement.
Yom Kippur is the first day of the Ten Days of Repentance.
Kol Nidre is a declaration.
Kol Nidre nullifies all promises of man to man.
Jonah was a prophet.
We eat Cholent on Yom Kippur.
We pray a whole day on Yom Kippur.

Draw a Line Under the Correct Answer

We chant Kol Nidre on: Passover, Yom Kippur, Rosh Hashanah.
The Marranos were: Spanish Jews, German Jews, Polish Jews.
Neilah is: the first service, second service, last service.
Jonah was: a merchant, a king, a prophet.
Nineveh was: in Assyria, Syria, Persia.
We blow the Shofar: after Kol Nidre, after Musaf, after Neilah.

Why

Why do we chant the Kol Nidre?
Why do we read the chapter about Jonah and the whale?
Why do we fast?
Why is it important to keep a promise?

General Questions

What is the difference between Rosh Hashanah and Yom Kippur?
Why is Yom Kippur so important?
Which promises does Kol Nidre nullify, and which does it not nullify?
Do you know of any instance when a broken promise hurt someone?

Sukkoth

HOSHANAH RABBAH, SHEMINI ATZERETH, SIMCHATH TORAH

The holiday of Sukkoth is celebrated from the 15th through the 22nd day of Tishri (September or October). It includes three other holiday celebrations: Hoshanah Rabbah, Shemini Atzereth and Simchath Torah.

Sukkoth means "huts." When the Jews lived in the desert after their exodus from Egypt, they gathered and dwelt in huts and tents. Later, when they settled in Israel, they again used small huts during harvest time. These field huts served as temporary dwellings to save valuable time and energy for the Jewish farmers. We therefore call this holiday the "Holiday of Huts"

(Chag Hasukkoth), as well as the "Holiday of Ingathering" (Chag Heasif).

SPECIAL SUKKOTH CUSTOMS

We observe the Holiday of Huts today by erecting temporary huts, and eating in the Sukkoth during the holiday. The Sukkah (hut) represents the faith our ancestors had in the Lord, that he would take them across the dangerous desert in safety. When we sit in a Sukkah, we express our faith in and reliance on God.

Because it is also a harvest festival and an agricultural holiday, we use the following four plants: the Ethrog, Lulav, Hadas and Aravah.

1. *Ethrog:*   The Ethrog is a citron fruit which grows all year on its tree, and has a good smell and a good taste. It symbolizes those individuals who are both educated and who do good deeds.

2. *Lulav:*   The Lulav is a branch of a palm tree which produces good fruit, but has no odor. It represents people with great wealth, but without good deeds.

3. *Hadas:*   The Hadas is a myrtle branch. It has a pleasant odor but no taste. It is used as a symbol for those people who are educated, but who do not use their knowledge for the benefit of the welfare of their fellow men.

4. *Aravah:*   The Aravah is a willow branch. It can neither be eaten, nor does it have a good smell. It represents people without education, without money, and without good deeds.

The Lulav is bound together with three myrtles and two willows. Then the Ethrog is held in the left hand, while the Lulav, the myrtles and willows are held in the right hand near the ethrog, and the blessing is chanted over the four plants. This denotes the unity of the different kinds of people represented by these plants.

The four plants are also used during the Sukkoth holiday in making a Hakafa (circuit) around the congregation standing in the synagogue. The cantor leads the procession, and each man who has a Lulav and Ethrog follows behind him. During the procession, the cantor recites the Hoshanah prayers, asking for blessings on the land and fruit of Israel.

Hoshanah Rabbah

Hoshanah Rabbah, or the great deliverance day, is observed on the seventh day of Sukkoth. In addition to a special service, there take place seven Hakafoth (circuits) around the synagogue. On this day also, a bunch of willow branches, or Hoshanoth, are used with our prayers. As we say a certain prayer, we beat the willow branches against the synagogue benches, to cause the leaves to fall off. This represents:

1. A symbol of the renewal of life—old leaves fall off in the fall season and new ones grow in the spring season; old generations pass on and are replaced by new generations.

2. A reminder of the Babylonian captivity. When the Jews were exiled to Babylon, after the destruction of the First Temple (586 B.C.E.*), they were commanded by their captors to entertain them by playing happy songs. Instead, the Jews hung their instruments on willow branches and refused to play while their Temple was being destroyed.

3. It is believed that on Hoshanah Rabbah, God delivers his final decision as to the fate of each person for the forthcoming year.

Shemini Atzereth

The eighth day of Sukkoth is called Shemini Atzereth (eighth day of the holiday). On that day we pray for rain in Israel. Since Israel is an agricultural country with a scarcity of water, by praying for rain we show our solidarity with the Jews of Israel. On Shemini Atzereth, we also say a special prayer in commemoration

* Before the Common Era

of our dear departed, the same as we do on Yom Kippur, the last day of Passover, and the second day of Shavuoth. This prayer is called Yizkor.

Simchath Torah

Simchath Torah, or Rejoicing with the Torah, is celebrated on the 23rd day of Tishri, or the day following Shemini Atzereth. On that day, Jews circle about in the synagogue seven or more times while holding the scrolls of the Torah. This circling is called in Hebrew "Hakafoth." Children carry flags with suitable inscriptions and all sing and dance, rejoicing in our great inheritance. Before the Hakafoth, special portions of the Torah, called the "Atah Haretah," are read by assigned people who consider it a great honor to be so privileged.

On Simchath Torah the reading of the last chapters in the last book of the Torah is completed and the reading of the first book is begun immediately. This signifies that the Torah has no beginning and no end.

We rejoice in completing it as well as in beginning it again. Every man and boy who has been Bar Mitzvah is called to make a blessing over the Torah. On Simchath Torah, even the small children who are not as yet Bar Mitzvah are honored by being called upon to make the blessing together over the Torah.

TRANSLATION OF BLESSINGS FOR SUKKOTH

FOR LIGHTING CANDLES

Blessed are You, Lord our God, King of the Universe, who has sanctified us with His commandments and commanded us to light the festival candle.

Blessed are You, Lord our God, King of the Universe, who has kept us alive, preserved us, and enabled us to reach this present time.

FOR TALITH

Blessed are You, Lord our God, King of the Universe, who has sanctified us with His commandments and commanded us to wrap ourselves in the fringed garment.

FOR THE SUKKAH

Blessed are You, Lord our God, King of the Universe, who has sanctified us with His commandments and commanded us to sit in a sukkah.

FOR ETHROG AND LULAV

Blessed are You, Lord our God, King of the Universe, who sanctified us with His commandments and commanded us to take the Lulav.

FOR WINE

Blessed are You, Lord our God, King of the Universe, creator of the fruit of the vine.

FOR CHALLAH

Blessed are You, Lord our God, King of the Universe, who brings forth bread from the earth.

SUKKOTH STORIES

The Most Valuable Merchandise

A great sage once traveled by boat across the ocean in the company of many rich merchants. During the journey, the merchants continually boasted about the beauty and quality of their particular type of merchandise. The sage, not to be outdone, also boasted about his merchandise and praised it very highly, but refused to reveal what it was. During the voyage, the ship was attacked by pirates who seized all the valuable merchandise they could find. However, they could find nothing that belonged to the great sage.

When the ship came to port, the townspeople gathered to welcome the sage, and honored him by offering him the position of rabbi. In time, he became very wealthy but never forgot his fellow travelers, the merchants, who had lost all their possessions to the pirates. "You see," the sage would say, "my merchandise was the Torah, which could not be stolen from me, and which proved to be the best merchandise of all."

Abbah Hilkiah

Abbah Hilkiah was the grandson of Honi Hamaagal, and like his great ancestor, he also could bring rain by praying to God.

Once, when there was a drought in the land of Israel, two sages came to him to ask him to pray to God for rain. Abbah Hilkiah was then working in his field. He paid no attention to the two men.

Towards evening, he placed his bundle of wood on one shoulder, his robe on the other shoulder, and his shoes he held in his hand. When he had to cross a stream he put them on. When he passed through thorns, he raised his garments. His wife came out to greet him upon his return. When they reached the entrance of his house, his wife entered first, he second, and the sages last. The sages sat down at a table, wondering at the peculiar behavior of Abbah, as he did not invite them to eat with him. Abbah broke bread, gave one portion to his older son and two parts to his younger son.

When Abbah finished his meal he told his wife, "Let us go up to the attic, I have something important to tell you." The sages, left alone, wondered all the more at this strange conduct.

When Abbah reached the attic he said to his wife, "Let us both pray to God for rain, here in the attic, so that the sages will not know that rain came because of our prayers, and they will not need to thank us." Abbah prayed in one corner and his wife in another. Rain came as soon as they had finished. Abbah then came down and asked the visitors, "May I know the reason for your visit?"

"We came to ask you to pray for rain," answered the sages.

"But the rain came down without my help," said Abbah.

However, the sages knew that the rain came because Abbah and his wife had prayed to God and they said, "We know that because of you the rain came, but before we leave, would you be kind enough to explain a few things?" Abbah agreed to satisfy their curiosity. "Why did you refuse to answer our greeting in the field?" the sages asked. "Because I am a hired laborer and did not want to waste my employer's time."

"Why did you put a bundle of wood on one shoulder and the robe on another?" they continued.

"The robe I borrowed and did not want to ruin it by putting wood on it."

"Why did you put on your shoes only when you reached a stream?"

"Walking on the road I could see the ground, but walking on the bottom of a stream there might be something that would hurt my feet."

"Why did you not invite us to break bread with you?"

"Because I have very little of it, and did not want to extend a false invitation to you."

"Why did you give the older son one portion of bread and two portions to your younger son?"

"Because the older one stays home, but the younger goes to school to study all day long."

"Why did the first rain cloud appear from the direction where your wife stood?"

"Because my wife gives bread to the poor and her help is direct, while I give money for charity, which is not direct help. Also, when our neighbors annoyed us, I prayed to God to remove them from our neighborhood, while my wife prayed to change their bad hearts into good ones. God listened to her prayer and we now have excellent neighbors."

The sages understood why God considered Abbah Hilkiah so great as to comply with his prayers.

QUESTIONS FOR SUKKOTH, SHEMINI ATZERETH, SIMCHATH TORAH

True or False

Sukkoth is the Jewish Arbor Day.
Sukkoth is the Jewish Thanksgiving Day.
Sukkoth commemorates the exodus from Egypt.
Sukkoth means "huts."
Sukkoth is in the month of Nissan.
Hoshanah Rabbah is the 8th day of Sukkoth.
Shemini Atzereth is the 8th day of Sukkoth.
On Simchath Torah we make Hakafoth (rounds).
Atah Haretah is a blessing.
We eat in sukkoth seven days.

Why

Why do we eat in sukkoth on the Sukkoth holiday?
Why do we call Sukkoth the holiday of Ingathering?
Why do we rejoice on Simchath Torah?
Why do we make a joint blessing over the Lulav, Ethrog, Aravah and Hadas?

When

When do we celebrate Sukkoth?
When do we celebrate Hoshanah Rabbah?
When do we celebrate Shemini Atzereth?
When do we chant a special prayer for rain?
When do we celebrate Simchath Torah?

What Are the Following

Hakafoth, Atah Haretah, Hoshanoth, sukkoth, Lulav, Aravim, Hadas, Ethrog, Chag Heasif, Tishri?

General Questions

Why is Sukkoth so important to the Jews of Israel and to the Jews
all over the world?

Why should we Jews constantly think about the land of Israel?

Why is Israel important to the Jews of the world?

Why are the Jews of the world important to Israel?

Could you show some connection between each holiday in the
Jewish calendar and the land of Israel?

How do you observe Sukkoth, Simchath Torah?

Chanukah

The holiday of Chanukah is celebrated for eight days from the 25th day of the Hebrew month of Kislev (December) to the second day of the Hebrew month of Teveth (December). Chanukah celebrates the victory of the Jews over the Greeks in the time of the Second Temple, and the regaining of Jewish independence and the right to practice the Jewish religion. This holiday has two names—Chanukah, and the Holiday of Lights. The word Chanukah can be divided into two Hebrew words:

Chanu means they rested;

Kah in Hebrew numbers equals 25.

The Jews rested on the 25th day of Kislev from their battles against the Greeks.

It is called the Holiday of Lights because the Temple lamp was lit in Jerusalem for eight days, and this we do also during our celebration of this holiday.

The Story of Chanukah

In 160 B.C.E., the Jews lived in Palestine and the Second Temple stood in Jerusalem. The Jews were ruled at that time by Syrian Greek King Antiochus. He tried to force the Jews to stop believing in their God, to change their traditions and customs, and worship the many gods of the Greeks. The Jews refused, and rebelled against him. The revolt was led by the eighty-year-old Kohen (priest) Mattathias, the Hasmonean, and his five brave sons. Mattathias died soon after the beginning of the revolt, and his son Judah the Maccabee (the Hammer) became the leader. He defeated the Greeks in many battles, then drove them out of Judea, and once more the Jews were free in their own land.

The first wish of the Jews then was to relight the Menorah in the Temple in Jerusalem. To do this, they needed pure oil especially prepared for this purpose.

They first cleaned up the Temple which had been neglected and made unclean by the Greeks during the war. Then they searched for the oil necessary to light the Menorah. They found only a small jug of oil which bore the seal of the Kohen Gadol (High Priest), stating that it was pure. The oil in the jug was enough, however, for only one day, and it would take eight days to make pure oil. The Menorah was lit with this small amount of oil, and miraculously remained lit for eight days. In memory of this miracle, we light candles each year for the eight days of Chanukah.

HEROES OF CHANUKAH

1. MATTATHIAS   The old priest who started the revolt against the Greeks.
2. JUDAH THE MACCABEE (the Hammer)   One of the five sons of

Mattathias, who became the leader of the Jews after Mattathias died, and drove the Greeks out of Judea. Judah was also called the "Maccabee" because on his battle flag were the letters M-K-B-Y, an abbreviation of the Hebrew words Mi-Kamocha-Baelim-Adoshem, meaning "Who is like Thee among the gods, oh Lord?"

3. ELIEZER A priest who was killed by the Greeks because he refused to eat non-kosher food.

4. HANNAH Her seven sons were killed by the cruel King Antiochus, because they refused to bow down before a Greek idol.

CUSTOMS AND PRACTICES OF CHANUKAH

1. We light Chanukah candles for eight days. We light the first candle on the evening of the 24th day of Kislev as, according to tradition, the evening is considered part of the following day and therefore all Jewish holidays begin on the evening before the day of the holiday. The first candle is put in the Menorah from the person's right, and an additional candle is added each night. However, the candles are lit from left to right to stress the importance of each day of Chanukah. A special additional candle is lit each night. This candle is called the Shamash, or server; it is lit first, and then used to kindle the other candles.

2. We eat LATKES, or pancakes, which are made with oil or other fats to symbolize the cruse of oil found in the Temple by Judah the Maccabee.

3. Children usually receive CHANUKAH GELT (money). They play with DREIDLACH (square tops), which have the following Hebrew letters on their sides: N-G-H-SH, an abbreviation of the Hebrew words "Nes Gadol Hayah Sham," which means "A great miracle happened there."

4. Plays about Hannah and her seven sons, Eliezer the Priest, Judah the Maccabee, etc. are presented by children to teach them how to be brave and good Jews.

5. Hallel (Psalms of praise) is chanted to thank God for His help to the Maccabees.

TRANSLATION OF BLESSINGS FOR CHANUKAH

FOR LIGHTING CHANUKAH CANDLES

Blessed are You, Lord our God, King of the Universe, who sanctified us with His commandments and commanded us to kindle the light of Chanukah.

Blessed are You, Lord our God, King of the Universe, who performed miracles for our ancestors in those days at this season.

Blessed are You, Lord our God, King of the Universe, who kept us alive and preserved us and enabled us to reach this season.

FOR EATING LATKES

Blessed are You, Lord our God, King of the Universe, creator of all kinds of foods.

CHANUKAH STORIES

Judith and Holofernes

In the city of Bethulia, there lived a pious Jewish woman whose husband was killed in the battle with the Greeks. Her name was Judith. One day, a Syrian general, Holofernes, besieged her city and was ready to destroy it and kill all its inhabitants. Judith asked permission from the Elders of the city to try to save the people and, at the same time, to avenge her husband's death.

In the evening, she took some wine and cheese with her, stole out of the city, and appeared before Holofernes. She offered to help him conquer the city. Holofernes, not suspecting anything, and thinking that Judith was willing to be a spy, agreed to this. She then offered him some of her strong wine, as well as some of her tasty cheese. Holofernes drank the wine and ate the cheese with gusto. This made him very drowsy, and soon he fell asleep. Then Judith cut off his head with his own sword, tucked it under her arm, and entered the city. In the morning, the Syrians saw their commander's head on the top of a pole at the gates of the city. They became very frightened, and the people of Bethulia attacked the confused Syrians and defeated them.

To honor the brave Judith, it has become a custom among Jews to eat dairy dishes on Chanukah to remind them of the cheese which Judith fed Holofernes.

(Jewish Folklore)

Latkes

A poor man once came home and told his wife that he had been to a rich man's home and had seen him eating latkes. "Oh, if I could only have some latkes," he said. "After all, it is Chanukah!" His wife answered, "I would like to make some latkes for you, but I have no cream."

"Well, make them without cream."

"But I have no butter or oil."

"Make them without butter or oil."

"But I have no sugar."

"Make them without sugar."

His wife conceded defeat, and made the latkes without any sugar, oil or cream—she made them just from raw potatoes. When the poor man tasted the raw potatoes, he spat the mixture out, and said, "I can't understand the rich people. How can they possibly like and enjoy food like this!"

Washington and the Chanukah Candle

The winter of 1777 in Valley Forge was a bitter one. We were all sitting and waiting, for what? No one knew. I was the only Jewish soldier in Valley Forge at that time. We were hungry and cold, and some were without shoes. Many soldiers cursed George Washington, but I believed that he was right. On a number of occasions, I had seen him walk at night among the rows of sleeping soldiers, look at them with pity, and sometimes bend and cover some of them, like a father covering his children.

I recall my father in Poland being forced to dress in a bear's skin and dance before drunken Polish nobles for their amusement. What an insult and shame to my noble father. As soon as an opportunity presented itself, I ran away to America, and joined Washington's forces. I prayed every day that Washington should be victorious.

Before I left my father's home, my father gave me a silver Menorah, and said:

"My son, do not forget to light the candles of Chanukah wherever you will be. They will light your way to freedom."

I always kept my promise to my father. When Chanukah came, while I was in Valley Forge, I took out my Menorah, lit the first candle, and chanted the blessing. The Menorah suddenly reminded me of my suffering parents, brothers and sisters, and my decision to fight for freedom under Washington became stronger. I sat before the Menorah and cried, as I remembered my father's house.

Suddenly I felt a soft hand touch my shoulder. As I turned around, I saw General Washington looking at me with inquisitive eyes.

"Why are you crying, soldier?" he asked. "Is it because of the bitter cold?" I suddenly forgot that I, a private, faced the commander-in-chief, and began to talk to him like a son to a father.

"I am crying and praying for your victory, General, and I am sure that we will win because we are fighting for a just cause. We want to bring freedom to ourselves and others."

The general shook my hand and thanked me. He then sat beside me and asked, "What is this lamp?" I told him about the significance of the Menorah, and that the little candle symbolizes the fight of the Maccabees for freedom.

Washington then said, 'You are a Jew, a son of the prophets, and if you predict we will win, we shall win." He shook my hand and disappeared in the enveloping darkness.

George Washington won. He later became the first president of the United States. The bitter nights of Valley Forge were forgotten. The only thing which I remembered was my meeting with George Washington.

However, I was sure that Washington had forgotten about the Chanukah incident a long time ago. I moved to New York City. One Chanukah night I lit my Menorah and put it on the window sill as custom demands. Suddenly a knock was heard on the door. I opened it and was astonished to see General Washington standing there. The President of the United States himself was standing in my doorway. What an honor! As he entered, he said to me, "I passed the street and saw the Menorah which resembled the Menorah in Valley Forge. That little candle and your words brought light into my heart on that fateful night, and I never forgot it. Soon you will be honored, together with the other Valley Forge heroes, by the Government of the United States."

That night the General received the Menorah from me as a gift. I was too excited to say anything as the President shook my hand, thanked me and departed with my father's Menorah.

CHANUKAH QUESTIONS

True or False

Mattathias was a young general.

Judah the Maccabee was the son of Mattathias.

Antiochus was a Greek king.

We eat Homantashen on Chanukah.

We light eight candles on Chanukah because of a small jar of oil.

Latkes are eaten on Chanukah because Sarah, the wife of Abraham made them for the visiting angels.

Judah lit the Menorah in the Second Temple.

We light eight candles on the first night of Chanukah.

Latkes are eaten because Jewish women made them so hard that their husbands used them as ammunition against the Greeks.

A Dreidel is a square top.

Judah was called the "Maccabee" because he was the keeper of the bees.

Hannah's children were killed because they did not bow to an idol.

Why

Why do we light candles for eight days on Chanukah?

Why was Judah called the "Maccabee"?

Why do we play with Dreidlach on Chanukah?

Why do we eat Latkes on Chanukah?

Why was Eliezer killed by the Greeks?

Draw a Line Under the Correct Answer

Kohen Gadol means: high priest, general, big man.

Maccabee means: Hammer, player, fighter.

We celebrate Chanukah in the month of Tishri, Elul, Kislev.

Menorah is an organization, lamp, city.

The Temple was in Jerusalem, Haifa, Tel Aviv.

General Questions

Is Chanukah observed because we are commanded to do so in the
    Torah?
Could you show the similarity between the Maccabean fight for
    independence and the fight of Israel for independence in 1948?
Why do you like Chanukah?
How do you observe Chanukah?
Why is it important for every Jewish boy and girl to celebrate
    Chanukah?
Do you remember the blessings over Chanukah candles?
Do you know what the four letters inscribed on the Dreidel mean?
What does the word Chanukah mean?

Tu Bishevat

ARBOR DAY

The Jewish Arbor Day is called Tu Bishevat. It is celebrated on the 15th day of the Hebrew month of Shevat (January or February). "Tu" in Hebrew equals "15" (Letter T=9, Letter U=6). On this day the winter season ends in Israel. The heavy rains come down no more, and the sap begins to stir in the trees. Though it is mid-winter in America, in Israel Spring is beginning.

Tu Bishevat is also called Rosh Hashanah Lailonot, The New Year for Trees. Tradition tells us that on this day, God decides which plants shall survive and which shall die during the coming year. This teaches us that trees and plants are living organisms, and we should take good care of them.

Tu Bishevat is sometimes called Chag Hanetiot (Holiday of Planting Trees). Young and old Jews in Israel go out to the hills and valleys on this day and plant tens of thousands of young saplings. They replant forests, and seek to change the desert and rocky hills into habitable, life-giving areas.

On this day, the Jews throughout the world collect and contribute money, and thus do their share in planting trees in Israel. A people who for centuries were foced to live in dark, drab ghettos where almost nothing grew, always found joy in Tu Bishevat. They find even more happiness in this holiday today, when the Holy Land is again becoming "a land flowing with milk and honey."

SPECIAL CUSTOMS OF TU BISHEVAT

Since Tu Bishevat is an agricultural holiday, it is customary to eat on this day those fruits which grow in Israel. We eat Boksor (carob tree fruit), figs, dates, almonds and raisins.

The Sephardim in Jerusalem spend the entire night of the 15th of Shevat in their synagogue. They read portions of the Torah and Talmud referring to agriculture in Israel, and the fruits that grow there.

The Chassidim pray on Tu Bishevat that the ethrogim (citrons) should grow beautiful and perfect for the Sukkoth holiday.

BLESSINGS FOR TU BISHEVAT

FOR ALL FRUITS

Blessed are You, our Lord, King of the Universe, creator of the fruit of the tree.

TU BISHEVAT FOLKLORE

Honi Ha' Maagel

Honi Ha' Maagel was a saintly man. Once when there was a drought in the land of Israel, the people came and begged him to pray for rain. No sooner had Honi finished his prayer than rain came down in torrents. The people begged him to slow down the rain. Honi prayed again, and the rain began to fall in a natural manner.

One day Honi happened to walk alongside a farm and he saw an old man planting a carob tree near his house.

"How long does it take for the carob tree to bear fruit?" asked Honi. The old man answered, "It takes 70 years to grow and begin bearing fruit."

"Then why do you plant this tree? Do you expect to enjoy its fruit? You are an old man now," said Honi.

"I enjoyed carobs from trees which my parents and grandparents planted, and I want my grandchildren to enjoy the fruit when I am gone," answered the old man.

Honi walked along. He felt tired and sat down to rest. He fell asleep, and miraculously kept on sleeping for 70 years. Grass grew around him and over him, protecting him from the sun and rain.

After 70 years, Honi awoke from his long sleep. He noticed a man picking carobs from the tree which he had seen being planted. Honi asked him, "Where is the man who planted this tree?"

"Oh, that was my grandfather," answered the man.

"So I was sleeping for some time," Honi thought.

Honi went to his home and inquired about his little son and wife. His wife was dead, and so was his son, but his grandson was alive.

"I am Honi Ha' Maagel," he said, but no one believed him. He went to the Yeshivah where he used to teach, and found sages discussing a certain point of law. One of them said, "In the days of Honi Ha' Maagel we could find an easy solution to every difficult question simply by asking him, but now we have difficulty in solving many points of law."

"I am Honi," said the old man, but no one believed him. Some even scolded him for showing disrespect for the memory of a great sage. Honi went back to the place where he had slept, prayed to God, and died peacefully in his sleep.

Some days later, his great-grandchildren, while playing in that spot, found the body of a very old man. They did not know that it was their great-grandfather, the great sage Honi Ha' Maagel.

The King and the Figs

Once a king passed through a village. He asked an old man who was planting a fig tree, "How old are you, my man?"

"One hundred years," answered the old man.

"And you expect to eat figs from this tree?" asked the king. Answered the old man, "Your majesty, if I live long enough, I may be able to eat the fruits of this tree. If not, I will at least leave figs for my descendants, as my parents have done before."

The king was pleased with his answer. After a number of years, the king happened to pass the same village again and found the old man still alive. The old man filled a basket with figs from the tree which he had planted, and presented it to the king. The king was pleased with the gift; he filled the same basket with gold coins, and presented it to the old man.

A jealous neighbor of the old man happened to find out about this. So he filled a big basket with figs and presented it to the king, thinking that the king would also fill his basket with gold. However, the king became angry and ordered his guards to throw the fruit in the neighbor's face. Heartbroken, the man came home and told his wife what had happened, and how the king had treated him differently than he had treated the old man.

His wife comforted him by saying, "You are lucky that they were soft figs and not hard lemons."

TU BISHEVAT QUESTIONS

True or False

Tu Bishevat means 20 days in the month of Shevat.
Tu Bishevat is the Jewish Arbor day.
On Tu Bishevat we eat Israeli fruit.
Tu Bishevat is called Rosh Hashanah for trees.
We plant trees in Israel on Tu Bishevat.

When

When do we observe Tu Bishevat?
When did the Jews first settle in Israel?

General Questions

What is the meaning of the letters Teth and Vav?
Why is it important to have the land of Israel full of trees?
Why is it important to celebrate Tu Bishevat?
Do you recall the expression used often in the Torah to describe the land of Israel?
Do you know the names of some cities in Israel?
Did you ever visit Israel?
Did some of your relatives ever visit Israel?
Did you ever plant some trees in Israel by contributing to the Jewish National Fund?
Did you ever count how many trees are near your home?

Purim

The festival of Purim is celebrated on the 14th day of the Hebrew month of Adar (February). In a Hebrew leap year, when there are two Hebrew months of Adar, it comes on the 14th day of Adar II.

The name Purim comes from the word "Pur" meaning "lot." Haman cast lots to decide which month and day would be best to exterminate the Jews of Persia. Haman's plot did not succeed. The Jews were saved on this day, and therefore we celebrate it as a holiday.

The Story of Purim

During the period 450—350 B.C.E., there was a ruler in Persia by the name of Ahasuerus, who ruled over 120 provinces and lands in which most of the Jews of that time lived. In those days, the King, a ruler of one of the most powerful kingdoms, often spent time in making merry at drinking parties with his friends. Once he decided that his Queen, Vashti, should come and dance before his friends, though it was not usual for a queen to dance before strangers. When Vashti refused, the King became very angry and decided to get rid of her, for fear the women of the land would follow Vashti's example.

Ahasuerus then chose a new queen by means of a beauty contest. Her name was Hadassah, or Esther, a cousin of Mordecai, a Jewish leader. Upon Mordecai's advice, Esther did not tell the King that she was Jewish.

After Vashti's dismissal, Haman the Amalekite was appointed Prime Minister, and everybody was ordered to bow down to him. He disliked the Jews, and especially their leader, Mordecai, because he refused to bow down to him. So Haman, his wife Zeresh, and his friends plotted to do away with all the Jews.

At a time when the King was very drunk, Haman persuaded Ahasuerus to sign a decree giving Haman permission to kill all Jews in the kingdom. Haman described these Jews as traitors, but in reality, they were the King's most loyal friends. The date for the massacre, the 13th of Adar, was chosen by Haman and his friends by drawing lots (which in Persian were called Purim).

Later, Mordecai by chance overheard two of Haman's friends discussing ways and means of poisoning the King. Mordecai hurried to inform his friend Harvonah, one of the King's officers, about the plot. Both plotters were caught in action and executed. Mordecai's noble deed was written down in the Book of Chronicles of the Persian Kings.

One night King Ahasuerus could not fall asleep. In order to amuse himself, he ordered that the Book of the Kings be brought, and that portions be read to him. It happened that the page opened first by the reader related the good deed of Mordecai. "Did this man, Mordecai, receive his reward?" asked the King.

The answer was, "No". Desiring to reward Mordecai, the King decided to ask his friend Haman for suggestions.

Hastily, Haman was brought to the King. The King asked him, "How should I reward the man whom I like best?" "Whom does the King like best if not me?" thought Haman. He said, "I would suggest that this man should be dressed in the King's clothes, be put on the King's favorite horse, and be led through the streets of Shushan, and a great lord should proclaim that this is the man whom the King likes best." "In that case, my friend," said the King, "go into the next room and you shall find the man who will receive this honor." Haman was very disappointed and astonished when he saw that the man was Mordecai, his enemy. Nevertheless, Haman had to obey the King's order.

While leading Mordecai through the streets of Shushan and proclaiming him the King's favorite, Haman passed his own house. Zeresh, Haman's wife, seeing the procession, was sure that her husband was being honored. Who else in the kingdom could be so honored besides the King himself? She thought that the one leading the horse resembled Mordecai, the enemy of her husband. She therefore spilled a pail of dirty water on the one who led the horse. She nearly fell out the window when she realized that Mordecai was the man being honored, not Haman.

After this incident, Haman made all preparations to get rid of the Jews, especially Mordecai, his worst enemy, on the 13th of Adar. After all, he had a document signed by the King himself. When Mordecai was informed about Haman's plot, realizing that time was running short, he decided to act fast. He sent secret directions to Esther to act quickly, to see the King and upset Haman's plan. Esther sent word to Mordecai to tell all the Jews to fast for three days and pray to God, and she would do so also, before she went to inform and persuade the King.

Esther invited the King and Haman to a private party. Haman was happy with this invitation. But his surprise was great when, at the party, Esther disclosed to the King not only that she was

Jewish, but that on the 13th of Adar, she might be killed. When the King heard this, he immediately commanded that Haman, his ten sons, and his henchmen should be hung on a gallows 50 cubits high, which Haman had erected in order to hang Mordecai. He also ordered that all Hamanites be killed on the same day that Haman planned to kill all the Jews.

Upon the suggestion of Esther, Ahasuerus appointed Mordecai, who once saved his life, to the post of Prime Minister in place of Haman. Esther and Mordecai then sent letters to all communities of Jews to observe the holiday of Purim on the 14th of Adar; and, to this day, it is still celebrated.

Ahasuerus the King, Esther the Queen, and Mordecai the Prime Minister, lived happily ever after.

SPECIAL CUSTOMS OBSERVED ON PURIM

1. The Megillah (scroll) of Esther, or Story of Purim, is read on the 14th day of Adar.
2. During the reading of the Megillah, the children make noise with gragers (noise-makers) whenever the name of Haman is mentioned. This is a way of booing Haman.
3. Three-cornered poppy-seed pastries called Hamantashen are eaten to symbolize the hat of Haman. Hamantashen also represent the feast that Esther prepared at which time three people, Ahasuerus, Esther, and Haman were present, and the fates of Mordecai, the Jews, and Haman were decided.
4. A special Purim feast (Purim Seudah) takes place in the late afternoon of Purim, and is one of the happiest of Jewish traditional customs.
5. Gifts are given to the poor (Matanoth Laevyonim) and gifts are exchanged between members of families and their friends (Shalach Manoth).
6. A fast (Fast of Esther) is held on the 13th day of Adar, the day that Haman was to carry out his plan to kill all the Jews.

7. Purim itself is celebrated on the next day, the 14th of Adar, when the Jews defeated Haman and his friends. During a leap year, Purim is celebrated on the 14th of Adar II.

8. The day after Purim is called Shushan Purim. It is celebrated as a semi-holiday in accordance with the custom of the Jews who lived in the Persian capitol of Shushan, and who celebrated Purim a day later, on the 15th of Adar.

9. Ad-Lo-Yodah is a Hebrew phrase used during Purim. It implies a happy and carefree celebration to the point where one is doubtful as to his sober condition. Literally, Ad means "till"—Lo means "did not"—Yodah means "know." According to tradition, the Jews were to drink and make merry on Purim. In Israel, a huge celebration called Ad-Lo-Yodah is staged, with floats and banners depicting the Purim characters and story.

TRANSLATION OF BLESSINGS FOR PURIM

BEFORE THE MEGILLAH

Blessed are You, Lord our God, King of the Universe, who sanctified us with His commandments and commanded us to read the Megillah.

Blessed are You, Lord our God, King of the Universe, who performed miracles for our fathers in those days and at this season.

Blessed are You, Lord our God, King of the Universe, who kept us alive and helped us reach this season.

FOR EATING A HAMANTASH

Blessed are You, Lord our God, King of the Universe, creator of all kinds of food.

PURIM FOLKLORE

The Magic Drink

Once, on the eve of Purim, Simcha the tailor was brought into court under the complaint that he had gotten drunk and created a disturbance in town by breaking windows in his neighbor's store.

The judge, who was well disposed, felt that a Jew had the right to start celebrating Purim ahead of time. However, for the sake of the record, he asked Simcha for a "valid" reason why he should not be detained.

Simcha answered, "I felt depressed on the eve of Purim, because my wife did not have enough money to bake hamantashen. To cheer myself up, I took one drink. Now according to our sages, a Jew who takes a drink becomes a new man. To celebrate my becoming a new man, I had to take a drink. Then, I and the other man had to get acquainted, so we each took a drink. Naturally, after getting acquainted, we had to celebrate our new-found friendship, and," Simcha concluded, "this is why I am here in court." The judge dismissed the case.

The Barber of Karzum

There was once a man by the name of Haman who was a barber for 25 years in the Persian town of Karzum. Haman was an ambitious man, and when he saw, after working for 25 years, that he remained poor, he decided to join the Persian army and seek adventure in distant countries.

Soon a war broke out and the Persians suffered defeat. The Persians fled into the wilderness where they felt safe from the victorious enemy. However, they suffered hunger and thirst, and many died. Haman, one of the fleeing soldiers, went around begging some food from the other men. No one gave him anything until he approached a Jewish soldier by the name of Mordecai, who gave him some water and a piece of bread. Haman felt so thankful to the Jew that he offered to become Mordecai's slave. He signed a bill of sale on a parchment, and gave it to Mordecai.

Finally, the remnants of the Persian army made their way home. Haman moved to Shushan and became a barber. Mordecai settled among his fellow Jews, and because of his wisdom and piety, he became their leader.

One day Haman, wandering in a field, found a treasure hidden behind a rock. He bought a beautiful palace in Shushan, and in a short time became known as the richest man in the city. He became a frequent guest in the palace of King Ahasuerus. The King liked Haman for his smooth tongue, and finally appointed him Prime Minister. Haman then decreed that all Persians must bow to him whenever he passed by.

One day, Haman spotted Mordecai in the crowd. Everyone bowed to Haman. Only Mordecai stood erect. Haman became frightened: What if Mordecai presented to the King the parchment which Haman had signed, claiming Haman as his slave? His days as Prime Minister of Persia would be few.

Haman decided to get rid of Mordecai, before Mordecai got him. He came before King Ahasuerus, and told him, "There is a nation among your vassal nations, which is different from all of us. It has strange customs and acts very suspiciously, praying to an invisible God. For the protection of your empire, we should get rid of them."

Ahasuerus, not a very clever man, and a lazy person who did not like to bother with details, left it to his clever Prime Minister to settle the question. Haman, right then and there, asked the King to sign a parchment, prepared in advance, which would give him the power to kill all Jews, including Mordecai, their leader.

And so the struggle between Mordecai the Jew and Haman the Amalekite began, and resulted finally in Haman's defeat.

Mordecai and the Three Students

When Mordecai learned about the decree, signed by the King, to kill all Jews, he became very upset. He walked through the streets of Shushan trying to decide how to help his fellow Jews. On the way, three little Jewish boys were walking calmly home from school. Their calmness impressed him, and he asked the first boy, "What did you learn in school today that makes you so calm?"

The boy answered, "I learned, 'Be not afraid of sudden terror, nor of the wickedness of the wicked, when it comes.'"

He asked the second boy, "What did you learn today in school?"

"I learned," answered the second child, "the sentence which reads, 'Take counsel, and it shall be brought to nothing; speak the word and it will not stand; for God is with us.'"

"What did you learn, my boy?" asked Mordecai of the third boy. "I learned the sentence, 'I am your Lord who will help you as I have done in the past, and I will carry you and will save you (in the future).'"

As soon as Mordecai heard this, his mood changed and he became happy. He felt that God had sent him a message through the mouths of the three little boys, and he was sure that God would save the Jews and punish Haman.

PURIM QUESTIONS

Draw a Line Under the Correct Answer

Esther's other name was Rachel, Hadassah, Miriam.
Mordecai was Esther's father, uncle, cousin.
Ahasuerus was the king, the prime minister, the butler.
The Megillah is a book, a scroll, a place in Israel.
Haman was a hay salesman, a prime minister, a scientist.
Vashti was a queen, a washwoman, a dancer.

How and If

How did you observe Purim last year?
If a girl, did you take part in a Queen Esther contest?
If a boy, did you ever take part in a Hamantashen contest?
What part did you ever play in a Purim play?
Did you ever take part in an Ad Lo Yodah celebration? Did you
   ever see one?

True or False

Esther was chosen beauty queen in Atlantic City.
Vashti lived in Persia.
Mordecai rode on the king's horse.
Esther was the wife of Ahasuerus.
Shushan was the capitol of Persia.
The Megillah is the story of Purim.
Purim is celebrated in the month of Nissan.
We eat Hamantashen on Purim because Moses gave the Jews
   Hamantashen when they left Egypt.

Why

Why was Vashti dismissed as queen?
Why did Haman want to kill the Jews?

Why did the King command Haman to let Mordecai ride on his
favorite horse?

Why do we celebrate Purim on the 14th of Adar?

Why do Hamantashen have three corners?

Why was Mordecai rewarded by the king?

Why was Haman hanged?

General Questions

Why is the holiday called Purim?

When is Purim celebrated if it occurs in a leap year?

When is Shushan Purim celebrated?

When is the Fast of Esther observed?

Why do you like Purim?

Why is it important to celebrate Purim?

Can you remember other historical events similar to the Purim
story?

How did you celebrate Purim last year?

How many Purim songs do you know?

Pesach

PASSOVER

The holiday of Pesach is celebrated for eight days from the eve
of the 15th to nightfall of the 23rd of the Hebrew Month of Nissan
(March or April). The first two and the last two days are full
holidays, when no work is done. The middle four days are called
"Chol-Hamoed" or semi-holiday, during which time work is permitted.

The holiday is known by the following names:

CHAG HAPESACH   The Holiday of Passover, because when the
last plague was brought on the Egyptians, Jewish homes were
passed over and not visited by the plague.

CHAG HAMATZOTH   The Holiday of Matzoth, because during

this holiday we are permitted to eat only Matzoth (unleavened bread).

Z'MAN CHERUSENU The Season of Our Freedom, because at this time the Jews were freed from slavery in Egypt.

CHAG HEAVIV The Holiday of Spring, which is the time of the year when the holiday is celebrated.

ECHAD M'SHALOSH REGALIM One of the three Walking Holidays. The three Walking Holidays were Pesach, Shavuoth and Sukkoth.

On each of the three Walking Holidays, each male Jew was commanded by the Torah to make a pilgrimage up to the Temple in Jerusalem. On each of the pilgrimages, a gift was brought. On Pesach—the Omer (first ripe barley). On Shavuoth—the Bikkurim (first ripe wheat); and on Sukkoth—the four kinds of fruit, and special sacrifices.

The Story of Passover

Passover is one of the most ancient Jewish holidays and is considered the Jewish independence holiday, since it marks the exodus of the Jews from Egypt about 1300 B.C.E., after being enslaved there for 210 years.

Our ancestor, Jacob, and his sons and their families, settled in the province of Goshen in Egypt, at the invitation of Jacob's son Joseph, who had become second in power to Pharaoh, the King of Egypt. However, after Joseph died and a new king had come to power, the Jews were enslaved, and harsh laws were passed in order to destroy them. The new king ordered the Jews to make mortar and bricks and to build treasure cities. He also ordered that every Jewish-born boy be drowned. However, the more he oppressed the Jews, the stronger they became and the more they multiplied.

During this period when the Jews were slaves, a Jewish boy was born to Amram and Yocheved, the Levites. They hid the boy for three months, so that Pharaoh's men should not find him. They could not hide him, however, any longer. So his mother Yocheved put the boy in a basket, and placed the basket in the tall reeds on the banks of the Nile River. It happened that Princess Bathia, daughter of the King, came upon the basket and found the boy. She adopted him and called him Moses, because she had taken him out of the water. Moses grew up in the palace of the princess.

One day Moses saw an Egyptian overseer beating a Jew mercilessly. He killed the Egyptian and saved the Jew, but he then was forced to flee from Egypt. He settled in the land of Midian as a shepherd, and he married a shepherdess, Zipporah, the youngest daughter of the priest, Jethro.

When Moses was tending his sheep one day, he saw a strange sight: a small bush was burning but was not being destroyed by the fire. When he came close to investigate, the voice of God spoke to him from the bush and ordered him to return to Egypt and save the Jews from slavery. Moses followed God's command and on his way back to Egypt, he met his older brother, Aaron, who accompanied him to Egypt. They both came to Pharaoh, and in the name of God demanded that he let the Jews go out of Egypt. Pharaoh answered their demand by increasing the hardships of the Jews. In return, God then brought ten plagues upon Egypt. They were as follows:

1. Blood (all water turned into blood)
2. Frogs
3. Lice
4. Wild beasts
5. Cattle disease
6. Skin disease
7. Hail
8. Locusts
9. Darkness
10. Killing of Egyptian first-born

When the tenth plague hit Egypt, the Angel of Death killed the first-born Egyptians, but passed over the homes of the Jews. Pharaoh, whose first-born son was killed and who, as a first-born, was in danger himself, called Moses and Aaron and ordered them to take the Jews out of Egypt. The Jews left Egypt as free people, and moved to the desert on their way to the promised land of Canaan. The exodus occurred on the 15th day of Nissan, in the spring of the year. In their haste to leave Egypt, the Jews took the dough with them before it had risen and become leavened. They baked the dough into flat cakes (matzoth) in the hot desert sun.

So the Jews were finally freed from slavery. However, as long as they had not crossed the Red Sea, there was always the danger that Pharaoh might pursue them and try to bring them back to Egypt. And this is just what happened. After the plagues were gone, Pharaoh changed his mind, and his army pursued the Jews. The Jews found themselves between the waters of the Red Sea and the army of Pharaoh. God then told Moses to stretch out his hand toward the Red Sea. Moses followed God's command, and the waters of the sea split in two, clearing the way for the Jews to pass on dry land. When Pharaoh's army followed in their path, the waters returned to their usual position, and the Egyptians were drowned. The Jews were at last completely free. They sang a song of praise and thanks to the Lord.

CUSTOMS AND PRACTICES OF PASSOVER

1. "Maoth Chitim" (literally, money for wheat) is given before Passover to the less fortunate members of the community, to enable every Jew to celebrate the Holiday of Freedom properly along with the rest of his people.

2. Since during Passover the Jew is not permitted to possess any Chometz (any food containing in whole or in part any of the five species of fermented grain, and/or dishes, containers and other implements associated with such food), he is required to effect a sale to a non-Jew of all his Chometz. This is done through an

agent, usually the Rabbi of the community, and is called "Mechirath Chometz," or the selling of the Chometz.

3. The ceremony of "Bedikath Chometz" (searching for Chometz) is observed the night before Passover. Pieces of bread are placed on the window sills. Then, by the light of a candle, the bread is brushed into a container with a feather. The feather and the candle are put into a bag together with the container; the following morning, the bag is burned ("Biur Chometz": burning of the Chometz).

4. Matzoth (thin cakes of flour containing no salt or yeast) are eaten during the eight days of Passover instead of bread. This commemorates the flight of the Israelites from Egypt. In their hurried escape, they took with them unleavened dough as part of their food supply.

5. On the first two nights of Passover, the Hagadah (from the Hebrew "L'Hagid", meaning "to tell") is read, recounting the story of Passover. The first two nights are called the Seder Nights (the Hebrew word "Seder" means "order"). Passover is celebrated according to tradition, and in the order prescribed by the sages. This order of procedure is indicated in the Hagadah. It is customary to recline during the Seder ceremony, which is conducted at a table set in a prescribed order. The first part of the Hagadah is read before the evening meal. Then there is an intermission for a holiday feast. After the meal, the Hagadah reading is completed.

6. Three Matzoth are placed on the Seder plate in honor of Kohanim, Levites and Israelites who did not forget their language, customs and traditions while in Egypt. The unity of all Jews made the exodus from Egypt possible.

There is another reason why three Matzoth are placed on the Seder plate. Ordinarily, on every holiday and Sabbath, two loaves of bread or Challoth, are placed on the table. These two loaves, called the "Lechem Mishneh" (double bread) are necessary to make the proper blessing. During Passover, however, Matzoth are used. Since according to tradition, we are required to eat from the "Poor Bread" on Passover, the middle Matzah is used for this purpose. It is broken in two; part of it becomes the Afikomen, which is concealed temporarily, and the remaining piece serves as the "Poor Bread."

7. "Maror" (bitter herb) is eaten as a symbol of the suffering of our ancestors in Egypt. Long leaf celery can be used for Maror in place of horse-radish. In fact, it is better than horse-radish, since celery is sweet first, then becomes bitter as it grows older. Celery can thus serve as a reminder of the sweet and bitter times that the Jews spent in Egypt. When the Jews came to Egypt in the days of Joseph, life was sweet for them, but later after Joseph's death, life in Egypt became very bitter.

8. "Charoseth" (a mixture of wine, apples and nuts) is eaten to recall the mortar which our ancestors used for erecting buildings in Egypt while slaves of Pharoah.

9. An egg and roasted meat are used to symbolize the Pascal sacrifices brought to the Temple by our ancestors when the Jews lived in Israel. The egg was chosen to represent the holiday sacrifice because of its special qualities. All other foods are softened by long cooking, but an egg becomes hard. So, too, with the Jews: the longer they suffered in Egypt, the stronger they became. An egg is also round, symbolizing the cycle of life and death, freedom and oppression.

10. Salt water is used as a symbol of the tears shed by our ancestors while in Egypt. The salt water also may symbolize the Red Sea which was crossed by the Jews after leaving Egypt.

11. "Karpas" (vegetable) is eaten to symbolize the growth of vegetation in the spring.

12. "Kneidlach" (Matzoth balls) are eaten either in soup or with meat dishes during the Passover meal. Kneidlach, or Matzah balls, are usually eaten on the Seder night as a symbol of the rocks which fell upon the enemy when Joshua fought the Canaanites. This event happened on the eve of Passover.

13. Parsley is dipped into salt water to symbolize the miracle of the Red Sea which separated. White Maror is dipped into the Charoseth to symbolize the bitterness of life for the Jews in Egypt.

14. A sandwich of Matzoth and Maror is eaten on the Seder night. This custom was introduced by the sage, Hillel.

15. The youngest member of the family asks the "Fier Kashes" (the four questions), requesting an explanation of the special acts that are performed on Passover, at the Seder table. In reply, the father reads from the Hagadah the story of Jewish suffering in Egypt, and the exodus from that country. The reasons Matzoth, Maror, and other things are eaten are also indicated in the Hagadah.

16. The story of the ten plagues is related. God plagued the Egyptians in order to compel them to free the Jews from slavery. When reciting the ten plagues, wine is spilled from our cups for each plague. This denotes that our happiness is not complete, knowing that human beings have been killed, despite the fact that they were our enemies. According to our Sages, we should not rejoice when our enemy is beaten.

17. Four cups of wine are drunk, symbolizing the four promises which God made to the Jews in Egypt. They were (a) "I Shall Bring You Out"; (b) "I Shall Save You"; (c) "I Shall Redeem You"; and (d) "I Shall Take You."

18. Placed on the Seder table is an extra cup of wine, often referred to as the fifth cup, from which no one drinks. This is in honor of the Prophet Elijah. The door is open to admit Elijah who, it is traditionally held, visits every Jewish home on Passover and blesses the people. Elijah was the most beloved prophet among Jews, and many legends and folk stories have been told about him. The fifth cup also symbolizes the fifth promise of God, "And I Shall Bring You into the Land."

19. The Seder meal is completed with the eating of the Afikomen (from the Greek word meaning "dessert"), consisting of the broken piece of Matzah which the master of the house concealed

at the beginning of the Seder service. It symbolizes the Pascal sacrifice which was eaten in the Temple at the end of the meal. It has become a practice for the youngest child to obtain the Afikomen and demand a ransom for its return, for we cannot end the Seder service without it. Children play an active part in the Passover celebration. God commands us to tell the children about the Exodus, so that they may learn to cherish freedom and be proud of their heritage and traditions.

20. At the end of the Seder service, songs are sung, the last of which is "Chad Gadyah" ("One Only Kid"). This is a simple song, the moral of which is that God is the Supreme Judge of the universe.

21. The Song of Songs, written by King Solomon, is chanted on the morning of Passover in the synagogue. It describes nature coming to life in the spring, when Passover is celebrated.

22. On the second day of Passover, the counting of the "Omer" is begun. (Omer was an ancient measure of grain). When the Temple stood in Jerusalem, the Jewish farmer would bring an Omer of the first ripe grain to the Temple to express his thanks to God. The Torah commands us to count 49 days from the bringing of the Omer on Passover, and on the 50th day to celebrate Shavuoth.

TRANSLATION OF BLESSINGS FOR PASSOVER

FOR LIGHTING CANDLES

Blessed are You, Lord our God, King of the Universe, who has sanctified us by His commandments and has commanded us to light the festival candle.

Blessed are You, Lord our God, King of the Universe, who has kept us alive and preserved us and enabled us to reach this season.

FOR TALITH

Blessed are You, Lord our God, King of the Universe, who has sanctified us by His commandments and has commanded us to wrap ourselves in the fringed garment.

MORNING KIDDUSH AND BLESSING ON WINE

And Moses declared the feasts of God to the children of Israel. Blessed are You, Lord our God, King of the Universe, who created the fruit of the vine.

FOR MATZAH

Blessed are You, Lord our God, King of the Universe, who brings forth bread from the earth.

Blessed are You, Lord our God, King of the Universe, who has sanctified us by His commandments and commanded us to eat Matzah.

FOR BITTER HERBS

Blessed are You, Lord our God, King of the Universe, who has sanctified us by His commandments and commanded us to eat bitter herbs.

FOR VEGETABLES

Blessed are You, Lord our God, King of the Universe, Creator of the fruit of the earth.

FOR FRUIT

Blessed are You, Lord our God, King of the Universe, Creator of the fruit of the tree.

PESACH FOLKLORE

Moses the Shepherd

One day while Moses was tending his flock in the land of Midian, he noticed that a little lamb was running away. He chased after it, but the lamb ran faster until it came to a spring and began to drink water from it. Moses said, "My dear little lamb, if I had known that you were thirsty, I would not have chased after you." Moses tenderly cradled the lamb in his arms and carried it back to the flock. When God saw this, God said, "Moses is the right man to be the leader of the Jews and take them out of Egypt, as he is a man full of pity." And so, as Moses was walking back to his flock carrying the tired little lamb, God appeared to him in the burning bush and commanded him to go back to Egypt and lead the Jews out of that country.

A Bad Dream

Pharaoh had three advisers, Jethro, Job and Balaam. One night Pharaoh dreamed that an old man, a giant, appeared. He took all the elders, magicians, and great men of Egypt, and put them on one side of a pair of scales, and on the other he put a kid (baby goat), and the kid outweighed all those Egyptians.

In the morning, the king called in his advisers, told them his dream, and asked them to interpret it. Balaam answered: "Your Majesty, the dream means that a child will be born among the Hebrews, and he will destroy all the Egyptians. Danger threatens all Egypt."

"What shall I do?" asked the king.

Jethro talked first. He advised the king to lighten the burden of the Hebrews because the God of Israel avenges all who oppress them. Job remained silent. Balaam, who hated the Jews very much, advised the king to destroy the Jews. He advised the king to throw all the new-born sons of Israel into the Nile river, until no men would remain among them.

Jethro, who spoke up for the Jews, was honored by becoming the father-in-law of Moses. Job, who kept quiet, was punished by God with pestilence and poverty for some time. Balaam, who opposed the Jews, was killed by Moses in the battle between the king of Moab and the Israelites in the desert.

Elijah the Slave

Once there was a very poor man who had a large family to support. It happened that several days before Passover, when most Jews were preparing for the Seder and the great holiday of Pesach, this poor man had nothing in the house, not even a piece of Matzah. He tried to earn some money so as to be able to observe the Seder like any other Jew, but he had no luck. He stood in a corner of the market place and cried. Suddenly he felt a hand touch his shoulder. When he turned around, he saw a stranger standing near him. "Why are you crying?" asked the stranger. "Because my children are hungry and I do not have even one *prutah* to be able to observe Pesach," answered the Jew.

"Then sell me as a slave, and with the money which you will receive for me, you will be able to celebrate Pesach," suggested the stranger.

"But how could I celebrate the holiday of freedom by taking away your freedom?" asked the Jew.

"Don't worry, just do what I am asking you."

The poor man sold the stranger to a prince, who paid 80 gold dinars for him. The Jew observed the Seder in style, and then used the rest of the money to start a business. He became a rich man.

The slave who was sold to the prince was asked by his master,

"What is your specialty?" The stranger answered, "I am a builder and architect."

"Then build me a palace, and if you complete the work in three months, I will give you your freedom", said the master.

The next morning the prince was surprised to see a beautiful palace standing on his grounds, completely furnished. The prince then gave the slave his freedom.

As the slave disappeared, the prince saw letters of fire spell out the words: "Elijah the Tishbite." The prince then knew that his slave was really Elijah the Prophet, who would, in time to come, announce the coming of the Messiah.

The Magician

In one of the small towns of Poland there appeared one bright morning a magician, a very strange one. He was dressed in rags, but he had a stovepipe hat on his head. He never ate and never slept anywhere. When asked where he came from, his answer was, from Paris. Where was he going? To London. By way of Poland? He suddenly disappeared and reappeared on the other side of the street.

One day he hired a big hall in town and performed unbelievable tricks. From his mouth, he kept pulling out all kinds of silks. From his shoes, he pulled live turkeys. He bent down and began to scoop up gold coins; he whistled, and rolls and breads began to fly in mid-air. He whistled again and everything disappeared. Even though it was before Passover, when Jews are busy preparing for the holiday, still they found time to come and see the tricks of the strange magician. Just like the magicians of Egypt, they thought.

However, we shall leave the magician for a few moments and turn to Chaim Jonah who was once a rich lumber merchant. However, times had changed and he became poor. There were many times when his wife Beila had to sell some of her belongings to buy food for themselves. Even though they had no children, they suffered greatly. Chaim and Beila, remembering old times, tried to hide their poverty. They gave some of their hard-earned money to charity instead of buying food, so that their friends would not know the truth.

Sometimes Beila's neighbors tried to help her, but she refused, claiming that she had everything she needed. On Friday afternoons, she made a fire in her stove, even though she had nothing to cook, so that the smoke from the chimney should fool her neighbors.

When Passover came, Chaim and Beila drank the bottom of the cup of grief. They had no Matzoth, no wine, not even candles. Both sat in one room crying in the darkness.

Suddenly they heard a knock on the door. Chaim opened the door, and for a while could not see anyone in the dark. But he heard a man's voice asking permission to spend the Seder night with them, as he was a stranger and had no place to stay.

Chaim invited him in but explained to him that although he would be delighted to have him as a guest, unfortunately they themselves had nothing in the house.

Do not worry about the Seder," the stranger said, "I brought the Seder with me."

With a flip of his fingers, candles appeared in candlesticks of gold. He then motioned to the table in the corner. Chaim suddenly recognized the magician.

"Cover yourself, my dear table, in honor of Passover," the magician said. The table moved to the middle of the room, and from nowhere a white linen tablecloth appeared and covered the table. The stranger moved his hand, and the best foods appeared on the table. All Chaim and Beila had to do was to sit down and observe the Seder of Passover.

However, there was one hitch: According to law, you are not allowed to enjoy anything produced through black magic. The

Bible warns against it. Both decided to run to the rabbi's house and ask his advice, leaving the magician alone in their home.

The rabbi pondered the question, and then he said, "Anything produced by black magic could not be touched and handled, since all of it is just a deception and an illusion. Return to your home and see. If the Matzoth can be broken, and the wine poured in the glasses, and everything can be touched, it is not black magic, but Elijah the Prophet has come as a magician to help you."

When they returned home, they were overjoyed to find that everything could be touched. They realized that Elijah the Prophet had done all this for them. They were thus able to observe Pesach like all the other Jews.

(I. L. PERETZ)

PASSOVER QUESTIONS

Draw a Line Under the Correct Answer

Miriam was an Egyptian princess, the sister of Moses, a queen.

Amram was the father of Moses, his grandfather, his brother.

Aaron was the brother of Moses, his uncle, his son.

The Fier Kashes are four questions, four brothers, four sisters.

Seder is the name of a book, order of a celebration, name of a Jewish leader.

Maoth Chitim is charity, name of a place, name of a writer.

Bedikath Chometz is searching for Chometz, eating Chometz, burning Chometz.

Maror is the same as Charoseth, bitter herbs, sweet herbs.

Hillel was a great rabbi, first sandwich maker, wood cutter.

True or False

Passover is the holiday of fruit.

Passover is celebrated in Nissan.

Pesach is celebrated for two days.

We eat Matzoth on Pesach.

Moses took the Jews out of Egypt.

We celebrate Passover because the Jews entered the land of Canaan.

Elijah was a general.

Kashe means a question.

Why

Why do we drink four cups of wine?

Why do we put a fifth cup of wine on the Seder table?

Why do we sell our Chometz before Passover begins?

Why do we eat Matzoth on Pesach?

Why do we eat bitter herbs?
Why do we eat Charoseth?
Why do we dip twice?
Why do we put three Matzoth on the Seder table?
Why do we eat the Afikomen?
Why do we use hard-boiled eggs?
Why do we use salt water?

What is

Charoseth, Kneidlach, Seder, Fier Kashes, Maoth Chitim, Chad Gadyah, Karpas, Hagadah, Mechirath Chometz, Bedikath Chometz, Biur Chometz, Chometz, Shir Hashirim, Omer.

General Questions

Why do we celebrate Passover?
When do we celebrate Passover?
How many days do we celebrate Pesach?
Give three other names for Passover.
When do we start counting the Omer?
What is the Afikomen and why do we eat it at the end of the meal?
What is Chol Hamoed?
What portion of the Pesach celebration makes the biggest impression upon you?
Why do you like Passover?
Which part of the celebration do you like best?
Why is it so important to celebrate Passover every year?
Could you compare the Passover story to another historical happening?
How did you celebrate Passover last year?
Who asked the Kashes in your home last year?
Who conducted the Seder in your home?

What Do the Following Symbolize

Matzah, Maror, Charoseth, four cups of wine, karpas, salt water, 5th cup, Afikomen, Chad Gadyah, parsley, Passover.

Yom Ha'atzmaut

(INDEPENDENCE DAY)

The youngest of Jewish holidays is Yom Ha'atzmaut, Independence Day. It is celebrated on the fifth day of the Hebrew month of Iyar (May). This holiday marks the Athchalta D'Geula, beginning of the redemption, which was promised by God, and which religious Jews prayed for during the last eighteen hundred years. In our time, we were privileged to see how it came about.

The Story of Yom Ha'atzmaut

Ever since the Second Temple in Jerusalem was destroyed by the Romans in the year 70 C.E. (common era), and the Jews

95

were driven out of Palestine, the Jews mourned. Every year on the ninth day of the Hebrew month of Ab, they fasted, sat in stockinged feet in the synagogue, and cried over the destruction of their Temple and country. In their prayers, they recited, three times a day, the prayer "Vesechezena Aynanu B'Shuvcha L'Zion B'rachamim" ("May we behold Your return in mercy to Zion").

For more than eighteen and a half centuries, Jewish leaders like the great rabbi Rambam and the great poet Yehuda Halevi spoke and wrote about the rebuilding of the Jewish temple. They also went up to the Land of Israel to live there. Many were the false Messiahs that appeared during this time and said they would lead the Jews back to Palestine. But it was not till the 19th century that an organized movement began for settling the Land of Israel.

In the 19th century, anti-Semitic movements developed in Europe. This led to the development of the Chibat Zion (love of Zion) movement which was sponsored by the leading rabbis, Rabbi Zvi Hirsch Kalischer and Rabbi Judah Alkalai. This movement urged the Jews to return to Palestine where they could worship God without attack by their neighbors. Small groups of Jews began to settle in Palestine. Sir Moses Montefiore of England and Adolph Crémieux of France helped the Jews settle in Israel.

The growing hatred of the Jews by the European anti-Semites caused Dr. Theodore Herzl, a Viennese journalist, to interest himself in the idea of returning to Palestine. In 1897, he called the first Zionist Congress in Basle, Switzerland, which organized the World Zionist Organization for this purpose. Dr. Herzl travelled to see the German Kaiser, the Turkish Sultan, and other leading statesmen to get their help, but without success. He succeeded in interesting large numbers of Jews in the Zionist Organization, and they carried on his work after his death.

At the end of the First World War on Nov. 2, 1917, the leaders of the World Zionist Organization got the British government to issue the famous Balfour Declaration. It said that the British government favored the establishment of a national homeland for Jews in Palestine, and would try to help the Jews reach this goal.

The British army captured Palestine, and the British government was given the duty of developing the country and aiding Jewish immigration. Soon, however, the British found that the Arabs were opposed to Jewish settlement in Palestine. As the Jews began to develop settlements in all parts of the country, and to introduce new farming, new industry, new economic, cultural and educational undertakings, the Arab opposition grew into murderous attacks on Jewish activities. The British, too, were taken aback by the rapid development of the country, and often sided with the Arabs. To defend themselves, the Jews developed an underground army known as the Haganah (Defense).

The country grew, but relations between the Jews and Arabs became even worse. The British gave in to the Arabs, and often appointed Commissions to study the problem. After every investigation, the report that followed usually took away from the Jews the right to bring more Jews into the country, and to buy land for settlement. The Jews refused to accept these reports and brought in illegal immigrants.

The Second World War stopped this inner fight, for everyone was busy fighting Hitler. But after the end of the war, the struggle against Britain and the Arabs grew. The British then brought the question to the United Nations. On November 29, 1947, the United Nations voted to partition Palestine, and to set up a Jewish state in one part of it.

The Jews were very happy about this U. N. decision. The Arabs were very angry and began attacking Jewish settlements; the surrounding Arab countries of Syria, Lebanon, Jordan and Saudi Arabia threatened war as soon as the English left Palestine, and the Jewish state was set up. The English helped the Arabs by leaving them arms. They also announced that on May 15, 1948, they would withdraw all English troops from Palestine.

On Friday, Hay Iyar (the fifth day of the Hebrew month of Iyar)—(May 14, 1948), the representatives of the Jewish settlement in Palestine met in Tel Aviv and signed a proclamation setting up the State of Israel; 1,878 years after the destruction of the Second Temple, the Jews regained their independence.

At midnight of May 15, 1948, when British rule ended, the armies of the neighboring Arab states invaded Israel. A fierce series of battles followed, and the Arab armies were defeated and sent reeling in disorder to their countries. The U.N. intervened and drew up an armistice which put an end to the fighting. The entire world rang with praise for brave little Israel.

The rabbis proclaimed Hay Iyar as the religious holiday of Yom Ha'atzmaut, Independence Day, to be observed with special synagogue services and prayers of thanks to God, not only by the Jews of Israel, but by Jews throughout the world.

SPECIAL CUSTOMS OF YOM HA'ATZMAUT

1. If the fifth day of Iyar comes on a Friday, then Yom Ha'atzmaut is celebrated on the day before, on Thursday.

2. It is customary to dress in holiday clothes on this holiday, and to go to the synagogue for a special evening service on the eve of the fifth day of Iyar, and a special service the next day. The order of these services has been set by the Chief Rabbinate in Israel. Special psalms of thanksgiving to God are sung. Holiday candles are lit in the synagogue before the evening service.

3. Toward the close of the evening service, one long blast is blown on the shofar (ram's horn) and the cantor and congregation say aloud: "May we be privileged to celebrate this holiday next year in Jerusalem rebuilt." Then a short prayer is said for the redemption and rebuilding of all of Jerusalem and Israel.

4. Jews greet each other with the traditional holiday greeting, Chag Sameach—Happy Holiday.

5. After the evening service, a holiday feast is served, accompanied by songs of praise and thanks to the Almighty.

6. In the morning service of Yom Ha'atzmaut, special holiday hymns are included as well as Hallel (Psalms of Praise), which is said on all holidays. A special memorial prayer is chanted for those who fell in the Israeli War of Independence, and another prayer for the welfare of Israel. A prominent guest or the rabbi delivers the sermon of the day.

7. The luncheon served after the morning service is a festive holiday meal.

8. It is customary to distribute charity to the needy on this day, as a sign of our thankfulness and appreciation to God, the provider of the poor.

9. In Israel, Yom Ha'atzmaut is celebrated in the large cities by impressive parades, in which contingents of all the branches of the Israeli armed services participate.

TALES OF INDEPENDENCE DAY

The Happy Decision
(FROM THE DIARY OF AN EYEWITNESS)

That Friday, all Jews in Palestine sat glued to their radios. One question was uppermost in their minds: Will the U.N. in New York vote to divide Palestine into separate Jewish and Arab countries? I felt the tension wherever I went in Tel Aviv. No decision had been reached when the Sabbath came.

Saturday night—still no decision, and the radio announced that the session would most probably be put over to the next day. I decided to go to bed.

At one o'clock in the morning, I was awakened by the tooting of horns and shrieks of sirens. I dressed hurriedly, and went out to the street. Shouts were heard on all sides. "The U.N. has decided in our favor!"

I saw people hurrying towards the Great Synagogue on Allenby Road, and I joined them. In the synagogue, a capacity congregation was saying Hallel (Psalms of Praise) with great fervor. At the conclusion of the Hallel, I went out again to the street.

In the large square before the Mugrabi Theatre, young people in great numbers were dancing horas to the accompaniment of Hebrew songs. Elsewhere, large trucks crowded with young, excited people were cruising through the streets.

By three o'clock, I decided to get some sleep, knowing well that the celebration would continue all of the next day.

The next day, I rose early to go to Ramat Hasharon. On the streets, all cars were decorated with Jewish flags and bunting. There was no school, and young and old were in a festive mood, singing and dancing. British tanks which only a few days before had menaced passing Jews, now flew Jewish flags on their gun turrets. Children of all ages got free tank rides, and British soldiers were relaxed, joining in the fun.

The bus to Ramat Hasharon travelled leisurely through the crowded streets. On the outskirts of Tel Aviv, the bus stopped before a table creaking under bottles of Palestinian wine. Several men boarded the bus with bottles of wine and glasses, and each passenger was asked to drink and toast the important event. Strangers clinked glasses with a hearty "L'Chayim," and wished each other a Happy Holiday.

I had just entered the office of Ramat Hasharon, when a call came through reporting the first Arab attack on a convoy from Tel Aviv to Jerusalem. The first Jews had been killed, and the general alert was sounded.

The celebration in the colony continued. The school children were lined up in front of the school for the ceremony of planting two trees on this great holiday. As a guest, I was given the privilege of planting one tree. I felt deeply moved as my shovel filled in the earth around the roots of the sapling.

Later in the afternoon, returning to Tel Aviv, we passed an

Arab village on the move. The men, women and children were carrying their tents and other belongings. They were cursing and spitting in our direction. As our bus passed, some Arab boys threw rocks at it, but no one was hit. The rage and anger on the faces of those Arabs foretold the bloody fight that was ahead. But at the moment, every Jew was still overjoyed by the Great Decision.

I. M.

The Evacuation

The British army was being evacuated and tension increased. Contact with the outside world ceased. The Arabs were becoming belligerent.

On March 21, a small convoy left the village of Kvutzat Nitzanim. A few moments later, a terrific explosion was heard. The convoy had hit a mine. After this, contact with other farms ceased completely.

The Arabs began to shoot daily. The children learned to stretch out on the ground, as soon as shooting was heard, no matter where they were.

This life of terror lasted for weeks. Over the radio, the entire population of the village heard of the Proclamation of the State of Israel by Ben Gurion. Song and dance followed this news, which was suddenly interrupted by Arab snipers.

The next day, an order was received to evacuate all children from the village, as the Arab armies were rolling in from all sides, and they were known to kill every one, man, woman and child.

The children were prepared for a night hike. The mothers said good-bye to their children, and so did the fathers who remained to defend the village. Only the most experienced and daring young men and women led the children, the men and women carrying the babies, and the older children holding on to the small children. All walked in silence, listening to every sound, every rustle, because they knew that there were snipers all around. The men and women holding the babies watched every baby carefully, lest it cry or make any noise. From afar, shots were heard and rockets shattered the silence. There was complete darkness all around. One false step on the winding, rocky road, and the whole chain of children might be hurled into the deep below. The children acted like real troopers, for they realized their dangerous situation.

Finally, they reached B'er Tuvia. Warm homes were waiting for them. The children were saved.

The Fall of Gush Etzion

Gush Etzion was a cluster of religious colonies which protected the road to Jerusalem and to Tel Aviv against the Arab invaders of Israel. Even if Gush Etzion had not existed, that defense point would have had to be established by the Haganah. True, Gush Etzion finally fell to the onrush of the overwhelming Arab Legion, but not before it fulfilled its task of giving the other units of the Haganah time to organize the defense of Jerusalem and other important sections. By delaying action, Gush Etzion saved the Jerusalem area for the State of Israel.

On March 27th, 1948, Gush Etzion was established as the central point of defense for the whole Jerusalem district. Greatly outnumbered, with restricted supplies of ammunition, about 170 Haganah defenders formed the core of the defense. A plan of strategy was worked out, not only of defense, but of attack, to disrupt the enemy communications and thus delay their attack on Jerusalem and Tel Aviv.

The plan was very successful in the beginning, until the British began to help the Arabs in their activities. On May 4, 1948, eleven days before the end of the British mandate over Palestine, heavy artillery directed by British officers in the Arab Legion began to shell the Haganah positions, and this bombardment was followed by many British Sherman tanks trying to break through to Gush Etzion.

The Haganah defenders realized the importance of their position, and decided to hold out to the last man. Many defenders were killed or wounded, but the post remained in the hands of the Haganah.

On May 12, two days before the expiration of the British Mandate over Palestine, the Arabs, led by a British colonel, launched a decisive attack. There were over 10,000 Arabs against 100 defenders. An armored column of the Arab Legion, after a heavy battle, reached Kfar Etzion. The enemy tried four times to break through to the center of Gush Etzion, but was repulsed with heavy losses.

The next day, twenty people with two Bren guns held out against sixteen attacks. Finally, the stand against the Arabs, led by the British, became desperate. The defenders decided to get the children out to a safer place, and then fight from house to house, knocking out tanks with Molotov cocktails (bottles filled with kerosene).

During the night, the children were bundled up and taken over difficult terrain to a safer place. The battle for Gush Etzion grew fiercer. To hold out further was impossible. The defenders contacted Jerusalem, and with its consent, signed a truce with the Arabs. They were taken prisoner by the Arab Legion, but not before they had attained their goal of giving the Jerusalem Jews a chance to conquer and hold the section of New Jerusalem for the newly established State of Israel.

Lag BaOmer

Lag BaOmer is a half-holiday celebrated by the Jews on the 18th day in the Hebrew month of Iyar (May). The meaning of the word LaG is 33 (Hebrew letter Lamed equals 30, and Hebrew letter Gimmel equals 3). LaG BaOmer means 33 days in the counting of the Omer.

Counting of the Omer

An Omer was an ancient measure of barley equal to a basket that held about 43 eggs. On Passover, the barley, which was planted in the winter, began to ripen.

Each farmer brought an Omer of this first ripe barley to the Temple on the second day of Passover. On the day that he brought the Omer, he would begin counting the Omer as the

Torah commanded him to do. He would say, today is the first day in the (counting of the) Omer. He would count 49 days, and the fiftieth day would be the Shavuoth holiday.

Lag BaOmer reminds us of the struggle of the Jews against the Roman rule during the 2nd century C.E. (common era).

Lag BaOmer is called the "Scholars' Holiday," because on this 33rd day of the counting of the Omer, the plague among the students of Rabbi Akiba stopped.

Lag BaOmer is also known as the Feast of Rabbi Shimon Bar Yochai. On this day, the Roman enemy was defeated and withdrew. Bar Yochai then left the cave in which he and his son Rabbi Eleazar had been hiding.

THE STORY OF LAG BaOMER

Rabbi Akiba

Rabbi Akiba, who was the leader of the revolt against the Romans, was an ignorant shepherd in his youth. He worked for a rich man called Kalba Savua. Savua's daughter, Rachel, fell in love with Akiba, the poor shepherd. She agreed to marry him on condition that he promise to study and become a learned man. Akiba, at the age of 40, went away to study in a Yeshiva for many years, and his wife Rachel lived in great poverty because her father disowned her.

Akiba became the most famous rabbi of his time, and he returned home with 24,000 pupils. The people of the city gave Rabbi Akiba a warm welcome. During the festivities, a poor woman tried to approach Rabbi Akiba, and his pupils wanted to stop her. Rabbi Akiba, however, called out, "Let her come near, she is my wife! Everything I know belongs to her because she urged me to study."

The Revolt of Bar Kochba

During the reign of the Roman Emperor Hadrian (117-138 C.E.), Rabbi Akiba, one of the greatest sages of that time, began a revolt against Rome. He chose a highly skilled commander, Bar Kochba, to lead the army, and Rabbi Akiba's pupils were the officers.

In the beginning, the revolution succeeded so well that the Romans left all of Judea, Samaria and Galilee in the hands of the rebels. But after several years of independence, the Bar Kochba revolution was crushed by Hadrian's general, Julius Severus.

The defeat of Bar Kochba was brought about by two causes. First, there were spies and traitors in Palestine who betrayed the country to the Romans. Secondly, a plague started, and every day a large number of Rabbi Akiba's pupils died. Only on the 33rd day of the counting of the Omer, the plague stopped.

Because of the plague, the army lost many leaders. Finally, the country was reconquered by the Romans.

Rabbi Shimon Bar Yochai

During this period, the Romans wanted the Jews to worship Roman gods, and not to teach the Jewish religion. The great sage Rabbi Shimon Bar Yochai, also known as Bar Yochai, defied the Romans and organized schools for Jewish children. There he and his son, Rabbi Eleazar, taught the Torah. The Romans found out about this and tried to catch and kill them. Bar Yochai and his son ran away and hid in a cave for 12 years.

Miraculously, a carob tree grew in front of the cave, and a spring of water appeared. So they ate carobs and drank the water while they studied the Torah.

Their little pupils would come to visit them, to bring them food, and study with them. In order to fool the Romans, the Jewish children took with them bows and arrows and baskets of food, so that it would seem they were going on a picnic. This is why it is a custom for Jewish children to go on picnics on Lag BaOmer.

One day, Bar Yochai saw a bird escape from a net. He took it as a sign from God that the Emperor was dead and they could return home. When they returned, they found that the symbol of the bird and the net had truly foretold their fate.

SPECIAL CUSTOMS FOR LAG BaOMER

1. The days of the counting of the Omer are considered sad days, and no parties or weddings are permitted during this period. However, on Lag BaOmer there are usually many weddings and other celebrations that could not take place on the other days.
2. Picnics and outings are arranged for Hebrew schools and Jewish children on Lag BaOmer. This is done in memory of the trips that Jewish children made to Bar Yochai's cave to study Torah.
3. In Israel, tens of thousands of Jews make a pilgrimage to Miron, a village in the hills of Safed. There, at the grave of the great Rabbi Shimon Bar Yochai, they pray, sing and dance. They make a great bonfire in memory of Bar Yochai and keep it burning all night while they sing and dance.

LAG BaOMER FOLKLORE

The Emperor Hadrian

Once, when Emperor Hadrian (who fought against Bar Kochba) passed along the street, a Jew greeted him. So Hadrian ordered the Jew to be killed because the Jew dared to talk to him.

On another occasion, another Jew who met Hadrian, knowing that one Jew was killed because he had greeted Hadrian, stood silent. Hadrian ordered that Jew be killed because he did not greet him.

When Hadrian was asked why he killed this Jew, he answered, "I am interested in killing all Jews, and no matter what they do I'll find an excuse to kill them."

The Death of Rabbi Akiba

After the Roman Emperor Hadrian crushed the Bar Kochba revolt, he began to hunt even more for Rabbi Akiba, who was the moving spirit of the revolt. In the meantime, Hadrian strengthened his decree that no Jew should study the Torah or teach it on pain of death.

A man by the name of Pappus came upon Rabbi Akiba as he was studying the Torah. Said Pappus to Rabbi Akiba, "Are you not afraid of the Romans that you defy their decree?"

Rabbi Akiba answered, "Let me tell you a parable. A fox once walked along the banks of a river, and he saw fish swimming back and forth as if disturbed or in fear of something. So he said to the fish, 'Why are you trembling so with fear? If you are afraid of nets or of other menaces in the water, come up on the dry ground out of the water, and you will not have to fear anything in the water.'

"The fish answered, 'You are supposed to be the cleverest living animal in the world, but you talk foolishly. If we are afraid for our lives in the water where we are at home, surely we should be more afraid on dry land where we will die for lack of water.' And so," continued Rabbi Akiba, "If we are in danger when we do study the Torah which is our staff of life, how much greater is the danger should we stop studying the Torah?"

Rabbi Akiba was finally seized by the Romans. He was condemned to death for participating in the revolt of Bar Kochba. Because he defied the Roman ban on Torah study, the Romans decided to punish him with a slow death. They combed his flesh with very sharp iron combs. However Rabbi Akiba did not utter a sound, but stood with a happy smile on his lips. His horrified pupils, who were standing by, wondered at Rabbi Akiba's calm behavior. They called out to their famous teacher, "Rabbi Akiba, how can you smile at such a terrible moment?" Rabbi Akiba answered, "All my life I wanted to be able to comply with the commandment that if necessary a Jew should give his life for God. Now that I am able to do so, I feel very happy." Rabbi Akiba died while saying the words, "Listen O Israel, the Lord our God the Lord is One."

Bar Kochba

When the Roman Emperor Hadrian oppressed the Jews harshly, they rose in revolt against the Roman Empire. The real hero of the revolt was Bar Kozba. Rabbi Akiba, who was the moving spirit of the revolt, was so impressed with Bar Kozba that he gave him the name of Bar Kochba, meaning a star (Kochav in Hebrew).

Bar Kochba was such a powerful man that he used to throw back with his knees the large stones which the Romans hurled at the Jews by means of throwing machines (catapults).

Thousands of Jews from different countries came to Bar Kochba to enlist in his army. But Bar Kochba did not accept everyone. He would test every recruit first. If an applicant would without complaint have his thumb cut off, he would be eligible for the army of Bar Kochba. The result was that the sages complained that Bar Kochba was maiming thousands of Jews. Instead, they suggested that the test should consist of uprooting a cedar tree while riding on a horse.

Bar Kochba followed the advice of the sages, and he eventually had 200,000 soldiers who could uproot a tree while riding on a horse.

Bar Kochba defeated the Roman army sent against him, and Hadrian felt that Bar Kochba, of the small country of Judea, was becoming a real menace to Rome. He summoned Severus, his best general, to fight against Bar Kochba. Severus realized that in open battle Bar Kochba would defeat him as he had defeated other Roman generals, but in delaying battles, he might win. His tactics were successful. Finally, Bar Kochba retreated to Betar, a stronghold in the mountains where the Romans could never get him, and where Bar Kochba could stay for years. Hadrian was about to give up and return to Rome. However, something happened which changed his plans.

In Betar, there lived a pious man by the name of Eliezer. He would pray to God every day that Betar should not fall into the hands of the Romans, and it was said that, because of him, Betar held out.

A traitor, a Samaritan who wanted the Romans to win, approached Eliezer and pretended to whisper in his ear. Some people who saw them became suspicious of this behavior, and reported it to Bar Kochba, who demanded of Eliezer that he tell what the Samaritan had whispered to him. Eliezer, who had hardly noticed the Samaritan because he was absorbed in prayer, replied that he did not know what this was all about.

Enraged, Bar Kochba ordered Eliezer killed, because he suspected him of treachery. As soon as Eliezer died, the Romans found a way to enter Betar. Soon a soldier found the body of Bar Kochba. When it was examined, they found a snake curled around it. It was a snake that killed Bar Kochba, not the Romans.

Most of the Jews of Betar were killed, and the revolt was

crushed. However, a number of Jews hid in mountain caves from which the Romans could not dislodge them. Only last year, these caves were discovered, and many utensils and scrolls of those Bar Kochba soldiers were found.

LAG BaOMER QUESTIONS

True or False

Rabbi Akiba was a great rabbi.
Bar Kochba was a Roman general.
Bar Yochai fought against the Romans.
The Romans called Judea Palestine.

Why

Why did the Jews revolt against the Romans?
Why did Rabbi Akiba choose Bar Kochba to lead the Jews?
Why did Rabbi Shimon Bar Yochai hide in a cave?
Why did the Romans change the name of Judea to Palestine?
Why did Bar Kochba fail?
Why is the holiday called Lag BaOmer?
Why are no weddings allowed during the counting of the Omer, except on Lag BaOmer?
Why do we go on picnics on Lag BaOmer?

General Questions

What do you learn from the story of Lag BaOmer?
What would you have done if you would have been in Bar Kochba's place?
Do you go on a picnic on Lag BaOmer?
Why was it important for Jewish children to study the Torah then, and why is it important now?
Why is it important to celebrate Lag BaOmer?

Shavuoth

The holiday of Shavuoth comes on the sixth and seventh day of the Hebrew month of Sivan (May or June). The holiday has four names:

CHAG HASHAVUOTH   Holiday of weeks, because it is celebrated the day after completing the count of seven weeks since the Omer was brought on the second day of Passover.

Z'MAN MATAN TORASEINU   Season of the giving of the Torah. Moses received the Tablets of the Torah from God on Mount Sinai at this season.

CHAG HABIKKURIM   Holiday of the first ripe wheat. In ancient Israel, the Jews brought their first ripe wheat to the Temple in Jerusalem as a sign of appreciation for what God did for them.

ECHAD M'SHALOSH REGALIM   One of the three Walking Holidays.

Shavuoth was the second Walking Holiday, when all male Jews in the Land of Israel went up to the Temple in Jerusalem to celebrate the holiday, and to bring a gift.

The Story of Shavuoth

In the third month after the Jews had left Egypt, they arrived in the Sinai desert, and camped opposite Mount Sinai.

Moses then was told by God to gather the Israelites together and tell them, "You saw what God did to the Egyptians. Now he is ready to give you one of the most precious gifts ever given to mankind, the Torah. If you will obey his commandments, He will always be present to help you and guide you."

The Israelites answered, "Everything that God commands us to do, we shall do. 'Na'aseh V'Nishmah'—we agree to do even before we have listened."

Moses then gave the Jews two days to cleanse themselves, wash their clothes and prepare to receive the Torah on the third day. At the same time, Moses told them not to come too near Mount Sinai. From early morning, dense clouds covered the peak of the mountain, thunder and lightning were frequently seen and heard. The sound of the Shofar came very strong, and the top of the mountain was enveloped in fire and smoke. The Israelites at the foot of Mount Sinai stood in great awe.

Moses then went up alone on the mountain, and as he neared the top, a mighty voice announced the TEN COMMANDMENTS:

1. I am the Lord, your God, who brought you out of the land of Egypt.
2. You shall have no other god but Me.
3. You shall not take the name of God in vain.
4. Remember the Sabbath day to keep it holy.
5. Honor your father and mother.
6. You shall not kill.
7. You shall not commit adultery.

8. You shall not steal.

9. You shall not bear false witness against your neighbor.

10. You shall not want (covet) anything that belongs to another.

The Israelites standing at the foot of the mountain listened to these commandments, which contained ideals of justice, kindness, wisdom and peace, and agreed to observe them.

The Israelites returned to their tents and waited for Moses to come down from Mount Sinai. When he appeared, Moses was carrying the Ten Commandments incribed on two stone tablets.

The Story of Ruth

During the days of the Judges, there came a famine in the land of Israel. Elimelech, a rich man of the tribe of Judah, decided to move with his family to the neighboring country of Moab, until the famine in his own land was over.

His two sons met the two daughters of Eglon, the king of Moab, and fell in love with them. The two brothers married the two princesses, Ruth and Arpah. Elimelech died soon after his arrival in Moab, and his two sons died soon thereafter.

Naomi, their mother, remaining alone in a strange land, decided to return to Israel, to be among her own people. Ruth, one of the daughters-in-law, had accepted the Jewish religion in good faith when she had married Naomi's son. When Naomi decided to return to Israel, Ruth insisted on going with her in order to be among Jewish people, where she could practice Judaism. Naomi tried to dissuade her from following her, as Ruth had wealth in Moab, and in Israel she would perhaps have to suffer hunger. Ruth could not be made to change her mind, and she followed her mother-in-law, Naomi, to Israel. Arpah, Ruth's sister, did not want to leave her father's palace and remained in Moab.

Naomi and Ruth settled in Bethlehem, and Ruth gleaned ears

of grain in the fields outside of the city, in order to support Naomi and herself.

One day, Boaz, the owner of a field in which Ruth was gathering grain, happened to notice her, and fell in love with her. He learned that she was a relative of his and that she was devoted to the Jewish religion, and to her mother-in-law Naomi. He then married her.

Boaz was one of the judges of Israel at that time, and Naomi was happy to see her daughter-in-law Ruth being rewarded for her devotion to the Torah. Boaz and Ruth had a son by the name of Obed, who was the grandfather of David, the future great king of Israel.

Because of Ruth's devotion to the Torah, it was decreed to honor her once a year on Shavuoth, the day of the giving of the Torah, by reading the Scroll of Ruth, which tells the story of Ruth.

SPECIAL CUSTOMS AND PRACTICES OF SHAVUOTH

1. AKDAMOTH A poem in praise of God written in the Aramaic language, which is read on Shavuoth in the Synagogue.

2. MEGILATH RUTH (the Scroll of Ruth) On Shavuoth the beautiful story of Ruth, ancestress of King David, is read because David was born on Shavuoth. A Moabite princess, Ruth married a Jew in the land of Moab; when her husband died, she turned her back on a life of luxury to return to Israel and the Jewish religion with her mother-in-law, Naomi. She has become the symbol of loyalty and piety, because she chose a life of poverty in preference to giving up her religion and principles.

3. Synagogues and temples are decorated with greens and flowers, to remind us that this is an agricultural holiday.

4. Today Bikkurim, the first ripe fruit, are brought in Israel's villages and towns to special ceremonies, to express the people's thanks to God for all his gifts to them.

Special Dishes Eaten on Shavuoth

1. BLINTZES are a cheese pastry usually eaten on Shavuoth, the holiday celebrating the giving of the Torah and the summer harvest in Israel. They symbolize the Torah as being good as milk. They also symbolize the land of Israel which was once a land flowing with milk and honey.

2. MILK AND HONEY symbolize the land of Israel which the Bible tells us was a "land flowing with milk and honey."

3. SHALTENOSES are cold blintzes and are eaten on Shavuoth. This dish originated among the Lithuanian Jews.

TRANSLATION OF BLESSINGS FOR SHAVUOTH

FOR LIGHTING CANDLES

Blessed are You, Lord our God, King of the Universe, who sanctified us with His commandments and commanded us to light the festival candle.

Blessed are You, Lord our God, King of the Universe, who kept us alive and preserved us and enabled us to reach this season.

FOR WINE

Blessed are You, Lord our God, King of the Universe, creator of the fruit of the vine.

FOR THE TALITH

Blessed are You, Lord our God, King of the Universe, who has sanctified us with His commandments and commanded us to wrap ourselves in the fringed garment.

FOR BREAD

Blessed are You, Lord our God, King of the Universe, who brings forth bread from the earth.

SHAVUOTH FOLKLORE

The Modest Mountain

When it became known that God would deliver the Torah to Moses on one of the mountains, all the mountains began to fight for the honor.

The tallest mountain said, "The Torah should be given on me for I am the highest." The most impressive said, "On me the Torah should be given, for I am the most majestic." The craggiest mountain said, "Only I am worthy to have the Torah given on me, for I am lofty and inaccessible." Of all the mountains, only the smallest, Mount Sinai, said nothing.

Then the Voice of God was heard: "You all quarrel in vain. I shall not pick the highest, the mightiest nor the most impressive mountain, but the humblest and smallest mountain among you." And God chose Mount Sinai.

The Guarantors

Before God gave the Torah, he said to Moses, "The children of Israel have agreed to accept the Torah. However, I would like to have someone guarantee that the children of Israel will observe the laws of the Torah."

Moses told God's wish to the Israelites, and they answered, "Our ancestors, Abraham, Isaac and Jacob, will be our guarantors."

God answered, "Your ancestors lived in the past. I need someone who will give a guarantee now."

"Our prophets are pious enough to be a guarantee," said the Israelites.

"Your prophets may be good men, but they will not be strong enough to make you observe the Torah," answered God.

"We will then give you our children as assurance that we will observe the Torah," said the Jews.

"Your children are the best guarantee," replied God, and then commanded Moses to go up to Mount Sinai to receive the Torah.

SHAVUOTH QUESTIONS

Draw a Line Under the Correct Answer

Ruth was the mother of Jacob, the ancestress of King David,
   daughter of Abraham.
Naomi was Ruth's mother-in-law, her sister, her mother.
Omer is the name of a city, of a measure of grain, of a man.
Boaz was a farmer, banker, teacher.
Mount Sinai is in Israel, Egypt, Persia.
Shavuoth is celebrated in the month of Cheshvan, Adar, Sivan.

True or False

The Ten Commandments were written on parchment.
The Torah was given to Aaron.
The Torah was given on Mount Sinai.
The Torah was given on Shavuoth.
We make a blessing over the Lulav on Shavuoth.
Shavuoth is celebrated for ten days.
Shavuoth is an agricultural holiday.
We eat blintzes on Shavuoth.

Why

Why do we call the holiday Shavuoth?
Why is Shavuoth called the holiday of first fruits?
Why is Shavuoth called also the season of the giving of the Torah?
Why do we count the Omer from Pesach to Shavuoth?
Why do we read the Akdamoth on Shavuoth?
Why do we read the Scroll of Ruth on Shavuoth?
Why did Ruth and Naomi return to Judea?
Why do we honor Ruth every Shavuoth?
Why is Shavuoth important to each one of us?

Rosh Chodesh

The word month in Hebrew is "Yerach" from the Hebrew word "Yareach," meaning moon. This shows that the Jewish calendar is based on the orbit of the moon. The calendar consists of 12 months. In a leap year, it consists of 13 months, to even out the difference between the Jewish calendar and the general calendar, for our calendar contains 354 days, and the general calendar has 365 days. Some months in the Hebrew calendar contain 29 days, and others have 30 days.

The Jewish calendar as used today was finally adopted and arranged by Hillel the second, in 360 C.E. The names of the months are as follows: Tishri, Cheshvan, Kislev, Teveth, Shevat, Adar Alef, Adar Beth, Nissan, Iyar, Sivan, Tamuz, Av and Elul.

The word month in Hebrew is also "Chodesh," from the Hebrew "Chadash," meaning new. Rosh Chodesh means the beginning of the new month. During the days of the Temple, Rosh Chodesh was considered a very important holiday. The coming of Rosh Chodesh was announced by the blowing of trumpets. There were gatherings in the Temple, where special Rosh Chodesh sacrifices were brought. Families observed special Rosh Chodesh meals, and no work was performed on Rosh Chodesh. Even Rosh Chodesh candles were lit.

However, after the destruction of the Temple, Rosh Chodesh became a half holiday, where work was permitted. In the synagogue, however, at the morning services, Hallel is chanted, a portion of the Torah is read, and Musaf (additional) service is added. All this indicates that it is a holiday service.

At present, in the modern State of Israel, efforts are being made to revive the ancient glory of Rosh Chodesh. Schools hold Rosh Chodesh assemblies, at which reports of unusual achievements are given. Also awards for monthly achievements are presented. The award of the monthly flag for patriotic duty or for exceptional work for the Jewish National Fund is also made. Special Rosh Chodesh songs are sung, and the National flag is saluted.

It is customary to announce the coming of the new month on the Sabbath preceding Rosh Chodesh at the Sabbath morning service. The introduction to the announcement is as follows:

"May it be Your will, O God, our Lord and the Lord of our fathers, to usher in the coming month, so as to be full of goodness and blessing. God grant us a long life of peace, goodness, blessing, sustenance, health, respect, fear of sin, a life free of shame, a life full of prosperity and honor, of love for the Torah, a life in which the desires of our hearts shall be fulfilled for the good of all. Amen."

ROSH CHODESH QUESTIONS

Draw a Line Under the Correct Answer

Rosh Chodesh is the beginning of the month, of the year, of the week.

Hallel is a collection of psalms, of trees, of books.

The Hebrew calendar has 12, 13, 14 months.

The Hebrew calendar is based on the orbit of the moon, sun, earth.

Chadash means: new, old, black.

True or False

Chodesh and Yerach are the same.

Yoreach means the sun.

Chodesh is the name of a holiday.

The Jewish month consists of 28 days.

General Questions

What does "Rosh Chodesh" mean?

When do we observe the holiday?

How was it celebrated in ancient days?

How do we observe Rosh Chodesh in America?

How is Rosh Chodesh observed in Israel?

BODY TRICKS

Other books by Michael Powell

101 People You Won't Meet in Heaven
The Afterlife Handbook
Behave Yourself!
Express Yourself!

MICHAEL POWELL

BODY TRICKS

STUPID HUMAN PARTY GAGS

The Lyons Press
Guilford, Connecticut
An imprint of The Globe Pequot Press

Copyright © 2008 by Gusto Company AS

The Lyons Press is an imprint of The Globe Pequot Press.

Cover design: Allen Boe

Illustrations: Allen Boe, Istockphoto

Text design: Allen Boe

Library of Congress Cataloging-in-Publication Data is available on file.

ISBN 978-1-59921-439-9

Printed in China

10 9 8 7 6 5 4 3 2 1

Disclaimer:
Please note that all the tricks in this book are for entertainment pur-
poses only, and are performed solely at the reader's risk and anyone
stupid enough to be in the vicinity. The author and publisher will not
be liable for mild discomfort, personal injury, or death caused as
the direct or indirect result of involvement with the frankly absurd
and time-wasting suggestions contained herein. Neither will they be
legally responsible for any consequential, indirect, or special loss
or damage, such as being smacked in the chops by an aggrieved
victim. Furthermore, don't come running to us when you accidently
saw through your neck or stick a fork through your eye. Really, can't
you just follow simple instructions for goodness sake?

CONTENTS

CONTENTS

CONTENTS

INTRODUCTION

Your body is an amazing masterpiece of wonderfully designed organs, muscles, connective tissue, and various other fleshy bits. But most of us bring into play only a fraction of our bodies' potential.

Body Tricks is the beginner's bible of physical magic. It is packed with sensational bodily secrets to give you the edge in a range of diverse situations. Whether you want to win an arm wrestle, experience supersonic hearing, break bricks with your bare hands, or stop your heart from beating, this book will show you how. Its awesome advice, topnotch tweaks, and superhuman stunts are guaranteed to impress your friends and help you to become a master of the known universe.

Harness bucket-loads of your untapped capabilities with one hundred must-have body tricks, from super strength to psychokinetic illusions, and from gross-out chicanery to good, honest fun. Some tricks unlock mysterious powers, such as those found in martial arts, while others are simply unique ways to spend time entertaining yourself and others that you probably would've spent eating junk food or watching TV. Have fun!

⭐ UNBENDABLE ARM ⭐

There is a famous Taoist saying: "Learn to yield and be soft if you want to survive. Learn to bow and you will stand in your full height. To bend like a reed in the wind—that is the real strength." Here's a trick that perfectly demonstrates this philosophy, and shows how relaxation can generate greater resistance than tension.

1. Hold your arm straight out in front of you. Clench your hand into a tight fist and tense your muscles to make your arm as rigid as possible, like a piece of oak.

2. Challenge someone to try to bend your arm: One of their hands goes on top of your arm at the elbow crease, their other hand grabs your wrist. If they are about as strong as you, using a reasonable amount of force, they should be able to bend your arm at the elbow.

3. Repeat the challenge again, only this time you will use the power of relaxation and visualization to give you greater strength.

4. Hold your arm out, with a slight bend at the elbow. Relax all the muscles in your arm and allow your wrist to dangle. Use just enough muscle to keep your arm in the air. Feel the connection with the earth through your feet and legs.

5. Imagine that your hand extends out from you for hundreds of feet, but stay relaxed and don't move your arm. Fix your gaze on a tree or object far away and imagine you are touching it. The further away your target is, the better. If you have trouble imagining a long distance, start with a small challenge such as reaching across the room to flick a light switch, or to offer your hand to be kissed by someone standing several feet away (this one reminds you to keep your wrist relaxed).

6. Maintain this feeling. Have your opponent try to bend your arm at the elbow, like before, using the same hand holds.

7. If you are truly relaxed and your visualization is strong, your arm will be impossible to bend. You are harnessing a relaxed energy that becomes available to us all when we stop fighting.

This trick is often used on new initiates in martial arts classes to demonstrate that a new way of thinking and harnessing the life energy (known as Chi or Ki) is required for those who wish to look beyond the obvious to experience something more powerful in their lives.

BREAK BRICKS WITH YOUR HANDS

Breaking bricks with your hands requires impeccable technique and considerable mental focus. The three basic principles are believing in yourself, hitting the brick as fast as possible, and minimizing the contact surface of the blow to maximize force.

Stance With the soles of your feet making firm contact with the ground, bend your knees to lower your center of gravity. This is the solid base from which you can generate the power and speed to break bricks.

Intense focus Place both your hands on the surface of the brick, and focus intently on the point through which you intend to strike. Aim for a target underneath the brick, right in the dead center. Maintain this eye contact until your hand has smashed through the masonry.

Speed and fluidity Move fast and with natural ease. Raise your striking hand backward behind your head in a natural arc, while keeping your other hand on the brick. This is your backswing, and it focuses your energy and keeps you fluid.

Turn your hips away from the target, and then bring them back again to transfer this torque energy into striking force. Slice downward with a knife hand, strike as fast as you can in a natural arc, and tighten the surface of the hand as it slices through the surface of the brick.

As your striking hand comes down, drive the other hand backward in a circular movement to balance the body and to increase your power.

Contact surface The part of your hand that makes contact is the small bone just below your little finger (the fifth metacarpal). Human bone can withstand forty times more stress than concrete, while the muscle, tendons, ligaments, and soft tissue in the hand disperse the energy of the impact up through the arm, so that you do not injure yourself.

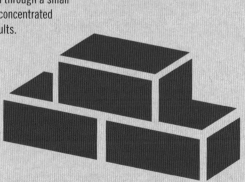

The more momentum your hand has, the more force it can generate, and when that force is delivered through a small point of contact, it is concentrated with devastating results.

ESCALATOR MIME

Convince your friends that there is an escalator behind your couch. This mime trick can be very amusing if you practice it sufficiently. You pretend to walk onto an escalator and descend out of sight.

Walk normally onto the escalator. Give a little jerk forward just as you get on, then walk forward smoothly, keeping your head level. Normally when you walk, your head will bob up and down, but if you keep your head level and walk smoothly, it will give the illusion of you standing still but being carried along by the escalator.

2. Now bend your legs smoothly and quickly as you glide forward, still keeping your head straight. The effect will be that you disappear out of sight as though the escalator is heading downstairs.

3. If you can manage it, casually turn your head to look out at your audience just before you disappear—it will crack them up.

You can do the same thing with a flight of stairs. Pretend there is a flight of stairs behind the couch. The way to make this convincing is to remember that when you walk down a step your body will remain upright. The only thing that will change will be the height of your head. You can control this by bending your legs sharply in stages with each forward step until your head disappears from view. You can then turn around and reverse the process to give the effect of walking up the stairs again.

The secret to all good mime is observation and imagination. If you want to convince someone that you are going to open an imaginary door, picture the door very clearly. How heavy is it? What is it made of? Are the hinges rusty or does it open smoothly? Is there a doorknob or a handle? If you really let your mind and body believe that you are opening a door, you will respond accordingly and the mime will be convincing. The more clearly you can see and live the experience, the more convincing the mime will be. Mime is not about showing off; it is about really living an experience.

LEVITATION

Levitation is a phenomenon of psychokinesis in which objects, people, and animals are lifted into the air, without any visibly physical means, and float or fly about. The phenomenon has been said to have occurred in mediumship, shamanism, trances, mystical rapture, and demonic possession. Here are two ways to achieve the effect of leaving your audience convinced that you possess uncanny powers.

Balducci levitation In this classic version of the trick, your small audience is behind you at a 45-degree backward angle, and they must be about eight feet away. Make sure you are wearing baggy trousers that extend to just above your heels. Place both feet together with all your weight on your strongest foot. Place your arms out to the side and begin to sell the fact that you are attempting to rise. To levitate keep your heels firmly braced together and rise on to tiptoes on your strongest foot, while raising the other foot completely off the ground, keeping the sole parallel to the floor. Hover for just a second, and then come back down to earth.

Balducci plus If the Balducci Levitation doesn't fool your audience, this version defies explanation. Standing with your audience to the side, you must slide the foot that is furthest away from them out of its shoe and place it down on the floor so that it is hidden by your other leg. You then sandwich your empty shoe against the other one and when you rise up on your bare foot, it gives the illusion that both your feet are lifting off the ground. The advantage of this method is that both toes can be seen clearly lifting off the ground, effectively ruling out the possibility that you are on tiptoes.

The moment when you take your foot out of your shoe and place it back again at the end requires masterful misdirection. The best way is to find a plausible reason to cover your legs for the second that it takes you to do this. If you take off your jacket, place it in front of your feet at the crucial moment and invent some business that distracts them like "other illusionists cover over their feet like this, but I'm not going to do that" (of course you just have—and that's the instant when you take your foot out of, or return it to, your shoe).

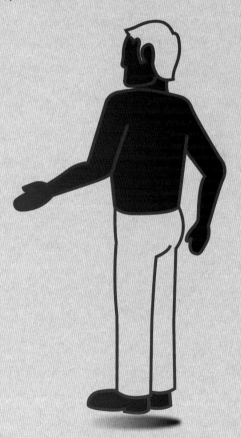

RIP A PHONE BOOK IN HALF

No one uses phone books any more, which means they are only good for one thing: showing off your freakish strength. When you've learned the secret of how to rip a telephone directory in half with your bare hands, you will look forward to the day when that big useless brick plonks down on your welcome mat. Remove the shrink-wrap, invite over a few important dignitaries, and get to ripping.

1. Grip the top of the directory with both hands, with your hands as far apart as possible, thumbs behind and fingers in front.

2. Before you start tearing pinch the pages into a V shape at the top center. Look closely at the edge of the pages. There should be air trapped in the V in between each page. This is good because it means that the pages lose the collective strength you would normally associate with lots of layers.

3. Pinch the corner of the V with your thumbs until it rips slightly, then while you push inward on the crease with your thumbs, bend the ends of the book down by rotating your wrists (left wrist counterclockwise and right wrist clockwise). This allows you to rip through the first fifty pages or so.

4. Bring your wrists back to their starting position, grip firmly again between fingers and thumb, and repeat, rotating your wrists to rip another bunch of pages. You should also feel your pectoral muscles being used if you are doing it correctly.

5. Repeat until you have ripped through all the pages at the top of the directory. Now simply pull the two sides apart to spread the rip vertically down the entire book.

While you are practicing, start with thinner phone books, and only use thicker ones when you have mastered the technique.

If you are too weak to rip a phone book using this method, you can cheat by wetting your thumbs. This weakens the first few layers of paper and allows you to open up a tear more easily. However, this is fairly easy to spot, so use with care.

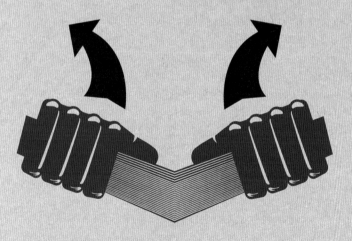

⭐ STOP YOUR HEART ⭐

Slow your heart down and then stop it completely—or rather, stop your pulse and make people think that your heart has stopped pumping (which mean's you're dead, doesn't it? Aaaargh!).

Here comes the science bit: The most common way to take a pulse is to place two fingers on the wrist, where the radial artery is located. Further up the arm is a large artery called the brachial artery that passes right under your bicep. In the forearm it branches into the ulnar artery and the radial artery. If you can constrict your brachial artery, you can stop and start your pulse at will to first give the impression that it is slowing down, and then stopping completely.

This is where your secret weapon comes in: a tennis ball. Hide one under your armpit beforehand. Have a friend locate your wrist pulse. When they are happy that they can detect a strong pulse, you can stop and start your pulse by squeezing and releasing the ball. What easier way can there be to convince others that you are one of the living dead!

⭐ SUCK A PAPER CLIP ⭐ UP YOUR NOSE

Get a medium-small rubber band and a paper clip. Put the rubber band around your palm and the back of your hand. Thread the paper clip into the band, and then hold the paper clip between your thumb and forefinger. If you let it go, the paper clip should instantly snap back, vanishing from sight. Now hold the paper clip and draw attention to yourself. When everyone's watching, stick the paper clip partly up your nose, then snort violently while letting it go. The rubber band will make it vanish.

Alternately, put a second paper clip in your mouth beforehand. After you've made the first one vanish, "cough up" and spit out the second one. Perhaps put paper clips in your mouth, both ears, belly button . . .

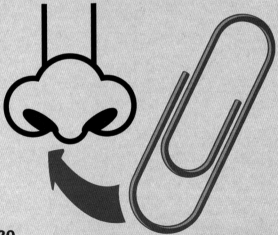

☆ SITTING PUSHOVER ☆

This is a martial arts exercise that is better known as "Kokyu Dosa." It involves two people kneeling facing each other. One gently holds the other by the forearm and tries to resist being pushed over. If you know how, you can push your opponent over with ease, and when it is their turn to push you, you can become as immobile as a mountain. The key is relaxation and mental focus rather than size and strength.

Both of you should begin facing each other sitting in a "seiza" position: kneeling on the floor with your legs folded underneath your thighs, resting the buttocks on the heels. Lower the tops of the feet until they are flat on the floor. Keep the back straight but not stiff.

Offer your wrists to your partner with your palms facing upward. Your partner holds onto your forearms gently. In order to guide them over onto their back, first you should raise your arms up in front of you while maintaining the feeling that your arms are unbendable (described on page 8). Then smoothly reach your arms forward and move your upper body forward by bowing from your hips. Keep your arms extended and gently push your partner backward and down. Stay very relaxed. Tension and muscle strength is the exact opposite of what you should be thinking. Think unbendable arms extending into the distance and relaxation with a powerful center (your abdomen) that gives you your core stability. Imagine your partner is a small child you can easily move off-balance. When your partner begins to move, guide them gently onto their back.

When it is your turn to resist being pushed over, use the same technique, gently meeting your partner's resistance by maintaining a straight back and imagining that your relaxed arms extend into infinity. It could take you months of practice before you see major improvement, but remember, if it doesn't feel easy then you aren't doing it right!

THREE FEATS OF SUPER STRENGTH

Here are three little tricks that make you appear super strong, all of which rely on using leverage to your advantage.

Immovable hand on head Sit on the floor and place your hand on top of your head. Challenge someone standing above you to grip your forearm at the elbow and attempt to pry your hand from the top of your head. No matter how hard they try you will win with ease, because if your forearm is a lever, they are holding it at the wrong end. If they gripped you by the hand, they'd find it much easier, but instead they are in the worst possible position of leverage.

Fingertip chair trap This is a great way to stick someone to their seat without using cement. Get your victim to sit in a straight-backed chair with their back pressed into the back of the chair and their feet flat on the ground. Stand in front of him and press your index finger into his forehead. Challenge him to stand up. He will be stuck in the chair, because to stand he must first move his center of gravity by bringing his head and upper body forward over his knees. He won't be able to, however, because every time he tries to bring his head forward, you simply apply firm pressure to his forehead with your finger to keep his head at the back of the seat.

Fingertip superglue This trick is like having your fingertips glued together so that no one can pry them apart. Stand well-balanced with your legs shoulder width apart with the tips of both index fingers touching. Challenge someone to take your wrists and, standing at arms length away from you, try to pry your fingers apart. Make sure they keep their arms straight. Unless they have awesome strength, you should be able to hold firm because you can apply leverage between your forearms and upper arms, while the other person can only use shoulder strength and no leverage.

360-DEGREE ARM TWIST

This deception was made famous by David Blaine (and invented by Shinkoh before him), but it is fiendishly simple to execute. Like many tricks it relies on some clever misdirection that allows you to set up your hand correctly. The effect of the trick is that you ask a spectator to copy your movements exactly. You proceed to place your hand on the floor and rotate it in a full circle, while your spectator will barely be able to twist theirs 45 degrees.

Invite your spectator to join you on the floor and ask them to copy you. Kneel down and place your right hand flat on the ground with the fingers pointing to the left and your thumb pointing toward your body. When they copy you, pretend they are doing it wrong and help them to position their hand correctly. Use this opportunity to get your hand into the secret position. Start with your hand palm up, fingers pointing to the left and your thumb pointing away from your body. Use your other hand to twist the hand 180 degrees away from your body until the palm is facing downward and the thumb is pointing toward you. Then place your palm firmly on the ground to keep it from slipping back. It might feel a little uncomfortable, but if you are fit and healthy your arm and wrist should be flexible and strong enough to accomplish this. With practice, you won't even need to use your other hand.

Make sure you are wearing a baggy long-sleeve shirt or jacket to hide the twisting of your arm. Your hand will look as though it is in an identical position to the spectator's. When you are satisfied that your spectator has his hand in the correct position, start rotating your hand counterclockwise. He will have to stop almost immediately, at which point you can enlist his help and ask him to guide your hand around slowly. Pretend all the while that you are really feeling the stretch. When your hand has completed a 360-degree rotation, if the spectator hasn't fainted with horror, push him over the edge by cracking the plastic cup hidden in your pocket!

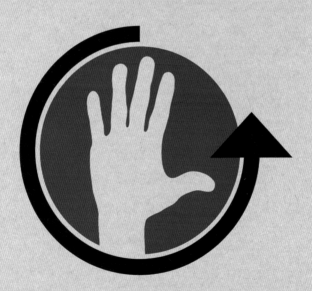

BODY ANCHOR

We all come from the earth and maintain a deep connection with its power throughout our lives—some people more than others. When you root yourself in the ground, your strength increases considerably, something that martial arts have exploited for centuries. This trick uses the earth to make you impossible to lift.

First demonstrate how easy it is to pick someone up when they aren't using this technique. Stand with your arms by your sides and challenge two friends to pick you up. They should hold onto your forearms (not your elbows) with both hands. Tense the muscles in your arms, and at a given signal get your friends to lift you off the ground. They should find it quite easy.

Repeat the experiment, only this time relax completely and imagine that your arms extend down the sides of your legs to the floor and beyond, deep into the ground (all the way to the center of the earth if this helps you to visualize). If this image doesn't work for you, imagine instead that you are standing on the edge of a cliff, and that two enormous weights are dangling over the cliff by ropes tied to your wrists. You are neither resisting nor pulling them upward, but simply allowing them to hang, while you stay completely relaxed. Don't look down—keep your eyes forward.

When you have established either of these images clearly in your mind and body, give the signal. Now when your friends try to lift you they will find it much more difficult, and with practice you should be able to become unliftable. Don't worry if it doesn't happen immediately; keep practicing and refining your thought processes, because strength always begins in the mind. And if you want to give the trick a comic turn, eat a pie or two between lifts!

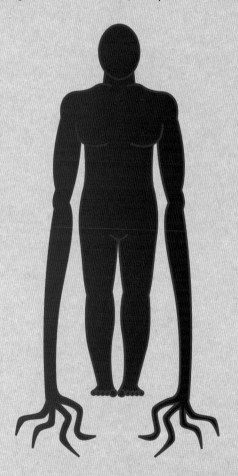

BREAK PENCILS WITH YOUR BUTT

Alex Mooney gets all the credit for this one, although if that's his real name it's too good to be true. This trick does exactly what it says—snapping pencils with your very own butt cheeks (with a little help from your undergarments).

Pull down your pants but leave your underwear on. This trick works best with loose cotton underwear, although just about anything will work so long as you can pull them up your butt crack.

Place the pencil across your buttocks so that it passes through the gusset of your underwear and comes out the other side. Now take a deep breath, pull your underwear tight (as if you are giving yourself a wedgie), and flex your buttocks to the max. As long as your butt has got a bit of muscle on it and isn't all fat, the pencil doesn't stand a chance. Mooney broke three pencils on *I've Got a Secret,* which originally aired on GSN, April 17, 2006. If, like Mooney, you ever get to do this trick on network TV, wear a pair of leggings to protect your modesty. If you end up with wood splinters, don't come crying to us.

DISLOCATED HEAD

The effect of this trick is that you get a pain in your neck, put your arm around the back of your neck to sort it out, sneeze four times, after which your head suddenly drops from your shoulders to end up in the middle of your chest. Anyone watching will think you've not only slipped a disc, but half a dozen vertebrae as well.

All you need to perform this gruesome stunt are two black shirts, one with a collar and one without, a black jacket, and a wire coat hanger. Lay the collared shirt out flat and carefully cut a large V-shape from either side of the neck down to a point at the middle of the chest. Squash the coat hanger so that it looks like a long sausage with a hook in the middle.

Put on the collarless shirt followed by the shirt you have just cut the V into and then the jacket. Place the long part of the flattened coat hanger across the shoulders inside the cut shirt. Now you are ready to perform the trick.

Approach an unsuspecting bystander and ask them if you can show them a simple body trick (pick another one from this book). In the middle of the demonstration, suddenly act like your neck is hurting and massage the back of your neck with your hand (this allows you to grab the hook end of the coat hanger). Then pretend to sneeze four times (ever more violently), and on the fourth sneeze yank the jacket and cut shirt upward by pulling sharply on the hook, and at the same time push your head downward through the V in the shirt. Your collar and jacket will remain where they were, giving the illusion that only your head has moved. You can even enhance the effect by hiding a plastic cup in your armpit and crunching it at the vital moment to make the sound of cracking neck bones.

Finally, place your other hand underneath your chin and heave upward as you lower the hook to return your head to its correct position!

WIN A STARING CONTEST

If you want to break into the big league of stare down, the following tips should help you to dramatically increase your chances of winning.

1. Immediately before the competition begins, keep your eyes closed tightly for several seconds; this will make your eyes water and help to protect them.

2. Stay relaxed. Stress will cause increased tension in your eye muscles, making them dry quicker. Also if you laugh or smile, you will be disqualified, so staying calm and focused will help you keep a poker face.

3. Try to make yourself cry during the competition by thinking of something really sad that has happened to you. Tears are the most effective way to keep your eyes moist.

4. If you think you are about to blink, frown to encourage the production of tears.

5. Don't let your opponent mess with your mind. No matter what mentalist shenanigans he or she comes up with, keep it real.

33

THE HUMAN ARMCHAIR

The human armchair is a tremendous gravity-defying ploy that relies on the cooperation of five friends. Place four chairs close together in a square so that they are almost touching and are all facing inward. The four people forming the armchair then take their positions. Each person sits sideways on a chair facing to the left, with their feet on the floor and their thighs at right angles to their calves (in other words they sit normally with their feet on the floor, with legs bent at the knees!).

On the count of three, each seated person leans backward, to rest their head and shoulders on the thighs of the person behind them, allowing their own thighs (which are still parallel to the floor) to support the head and shoulders of the person in front. Arms should be folded across the stomach (to keep them out of the way, since they aren't needed during the trick, and this also makes the trick look more effortless and nonchalant). Now a fifth person carefully removes the chairs one by one until all four are lying down luxuriating in the comfort of a human armchair, with no other visible means of support.

When you've all had enough relaxation, carefully collapse in unison into an untidy heap on the floor. If only human beings could be this much in harmony all the time, none of us would have any need for expensive furniture!

MAGNETIC FINGERS

When you want to demonstrate a little instant hypnosis, this trick is the one to choose. It relies on using your victim's strength against them.

Ask your victim to clasp their hands tightly together, with their fingers woven together. Encourage them to squeeze harder and harder. After about thirty seconds ask them to release the index fingers of both hands and point them upward an inch apart.

Now wave your hands mysteriously over theirs and announce that no matter how hard they try to prevent it from happening, their index fingers will come together and touch. Really get them to focus on their index fingers and challenge them to prove you wrong.

The beauty of this trick is that the harder they try to stop the fingers from touching, the more they will tense all their fingers and actually make it happen. Be patient. If their fingers don't touch within thirty seconds, it's because your victim has relaxed their grip. It is vital that they keep their hands gripped together tightly while focusing intently on stopping their index fingers from touching. Clasping tightly with the other fingers while simultaneously attempting to keep the index fingers apart puts so much stress on the muscles of the hand that eventually fatigue causes a momentary loss of concentration and/or strength. The fingers have to touch, and you become the inevitable winner.

PULL A THREAD FROM YOUR EYE

Some hardcore magicians do this trick the hard way: They swallow a piece of thread or stick it up their nose and then use a mixture of snorting and weird eye socket manipulation to pass it through their sinus cavities and out of their eye. Fortunately there is a safer and less gruesome way of creating this illusion.

First show a piece of black cotton thread, about six inches long, to your audience, then feed it into your mouth so that the thread passes underneath your tongue. Don't swallow it; keep it under your tongue and then remove it in secret after you have performed the trick. The trick stands or falls on what comes next: your ability to convincingly show discomfort. You are attempting to suck a thread up through your sinuses, so unless you offer up some well-timed hocking noises, followed by some, "I'm about to either be sick or sneeze" acting, your trick won't be as effective. Play around in front of a mirror and practice imagining what it would feel like to have a thread pass behind your eyes until you get this down pat. Feel it and you will be truthful, but don't ham it up or no one will believe it's for real.

In your other hand you have another identical piece of black thread rolled up inside your palm. Beforehand you will have dabbed a small blob of quick-drying eyelash glue (the stuff you use to attach falsies) onto the skin on the outside corner of your eye, making sure you don't get it in your eye.

Press one end of the thread firmly onto the glue until it sticks, and then gently unravel the thread hidden in your hand. Keep the thread that is visible taut, giving the illusion that it is being teased out of your eyeball. When you reach the other end of the thread, gently pull to release the stuck end from the glue and blink several times to make it look like you're trying to refocus.

That's how you pull a thread from your eye...the safe way. Whatever you do, don't use super glue or you'll end up in the ER with all the other numbskulls.

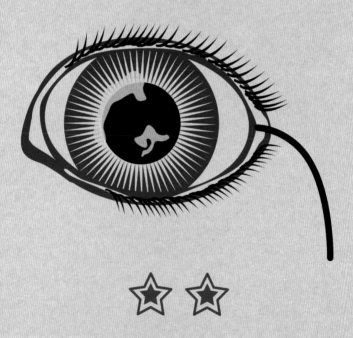

RING OF STEEL

In this amazing and simple trick, the aim is to make an OK sign with your thumb and index finger and then cement them so firmly together, in your mind, that anyone dumb enough to think that they can pry them apart will soon find themselves making a walk of shame. This trick is a simple demonstration of how much more effective relaxation is than brute strength.

The key to this body trick is to engage your mind rather than your muscle, although of course the end result is that your body responds in ways that you would have thought impossible. Relax your hand, by extending your fingers, then stretching them backward a little with your other hand. Now shake them out until they tingle slightly. You can also soak them in a bowl of warm water.

With your fingers gentle and relaxed, place your thumb and index finger together and imagine that they are spot-welded together, so that the O does not have any weak spots or joins. Your O is a solid ring of steel. Don't use your muscles—don't tense up to create the feeling of steel; use your mind. Take your mind away from the spot where your finger and thumb meet and are welded. Focusing on that point just exaggerates your weak spot instead that the joint does not exist; the O is a complete whole. Stay relaxed and use the minimum of muscle strength to maintain the solid, flawless O.

Now ask someone to pry your finger and thumb apart. Don't fight them by tensing up and squeezing. Keep relaxed. Ignore the challenge and focus on the seamless O. The more you practice this trick, the more you will understand that relaxation is the key to strength.

SAW THREAD THROUGH YOUR NECK

This trick gives the illusion that you are sawing a piece of thread into your neck. The thread appears to enter the skin, pass underneath it, and come out the other end.

Before you begin secretly apply a strip of rubber cement on the skin underneath your chin. Perform the trick with a piece of dark medium-gauge nylon thread about two feet long. Wrap the ends around your finger so that you can get a good grip, then place the taut thread against the center of the rubber cement band and begin to make a sawing action from side to side across your neck. After a few seconds drop your chin onto your chest (while feigning pain) and make a few groaning noises. You're puncturing the skin now, so it has to look like it hurts.

In fact what happens when you drop your head is that where the thread makes contact with your skin and the rubber cement the thread hides in the tiny fold of neck skin that gets glued together. When you lift your head again, it will look like the thread is underneath your skin, and you can move the thread from side to side, causing the skin to bunch at the entrance and exit points for maximum gross out effect.

To complete the illusion, remove the thread from your skin by gently pulling away from your body. This will pull the skin outward, further enhancing the illusion that the thread is buried beneath.

After the thread comes clean away, you can offer it for inspection and the rubber cement on your neck can be examined too, because it only sticks to itself and won't be sticky to touch.

WIN AN ARM WRESTLE

Arm wrestling does rely on strength, but there are lots of tricks most casual arm wrestlers don't know about, that can give you the edge. Let's face it, you're only going to have the occasional arm wrestle and are unlikely ever to meet a complete professional, so if you use the tricks below you stand a good chance of winning.

The first thing to sort out is the way you stand. If you are wrestling with your right arm, you should stand with your right foot further forward than your left. If you are a left-hander, keep your left foot forward. This gives you the maximum leverage and helps you to keep your arm close to your body.

Next comes the grip. Placing your index finger over your thumb (called "wrapping") helps you perform the "hook," which you should attempt in the first second of the bout. Snap your wrist toward you explosively to try to gain control of your opponent's wrist; once your hand is higher than his you have the greater leverage.

Don't just push sideways. Apply back pressure as well, bringing your fist toward your own body, which also takes your opponent's arm further away from his body, simultaneously increasing your leverage while decreasing his.

Every day spend five minutes doing power wrist curls to strengthen your wrist and forearms. Put some weights in the middle of a short barbell, sit down and grip both ends (try both ways, with palms up and palms down). Start with your wrists in line with your forearms and then curl your wrists upward as far as you can, and back down again. Repeat until failure (which should be about twenty-five reps). If you can't control the weight properly, reduce the weight, or if you have to do hundreds of reps, increase it.

Following these five simple tips will give you an awesome advantage over your opponent no matter what size he is.

BLOW SMOKE RINGS

Blowing smoke rings is about as sophisticated as you can get without quitting smoking altogether. It's not the easiest trick to master, but with a little practice you'll soon impress your friends with your cloudy halos.

First, it helps if you smoke cigarettes that produce thick smoke—ones with full-flavor tobacco or menthol. Before lighting up, pack the cigarette by tapping it repeatedly on a tabletop, pushing the tobacco closer to the filter.

Light up and take a few drags to get the fire going (these drags will have lighter smoke). Then take one big drag and partially inhale the smoke so that it stays in your throat. Close your mouth and bring your tongue to the back of your mouth with the tip pointing down.

Make a big pouty O shape with your mouth; really stick those lips out and begin to puff smoke out of your mouth in short bursts, as if you were making a "huh" sound (use your diaphragm, not your vocal chords). As the smoke leaves your lips, flick your tongue forward and sharply bring your lower jaw up a fraction.

You should aim to produce a tight, well-defined ring of smoke. The wider your mouth the bigger the ring, and the speed the ring travels away from you depends on the force you use to make your "huh" movement. Think of it almost as a silent cough. You're a smoker after all, so it shouldn't be too hard for you to imagine having one of those.

DISLOCATE YOUR NOSE

This is one of the simplest (and obvious) tricks you can ever do, but it still seems to fool most people most of the time, and it requires zero preparation. It gives the illusion of dislocating your nose from side to side.

Cup your palms over your face and grip your nose with your index fingers. Place your thumbnails behind your top front teeth (your hands are cupped, so your thumbs shouldn't be in view).

To dislocate your nose, sharply twist your cupped hands to the right and make the sound of cracking cartilage by snapping your thumbs forward so that the nails click off your teeth.

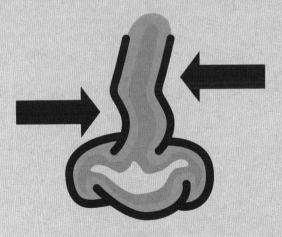

SINK THROUGH THE FLOOR

Here's a great trick for making someone feel as if they are sinking through a solid floor.

Have your volunteer lie face down on the floor with both his arms extended along the floor in front of his head. Pick up his hands and raise his arms and upper body about a foot off the ground. Stop if at any point it begins to hurt. Maintain this position for about two minutes and then begin to lower him down again very slowly. This part of the trick should take about a minute. As he sinks down, he will begin to feel like his head is lower than the rest of his body. Since his body is lying on the floor, his brain is going to get very confused, and he's going to feel as though he's poking his head through the floor.

You can modify this trick for Halloween. Dim the lights, switch on a flashlight, and inform your victim that you are lowering him into his grave!

STAGE FIGHTING

Here are five of the most common ways to fool a bunch of people into thinking you are really fighting. It is like a controlled dance, requiring practice and care to ensure that no one gets hurt for real. Also, it's probably not wise to show off your moves at the mall, or some public-spirited individuals might take it upon themselves to get in the middle of it.

The basic punch This works best when the viewer is standing behind the person being punched, and is least effective if they are standing to the side. Aim a punch to the air at the side of your partner's head (don't aim at your target or you might actually make contact). At the moment of impact, slap your chest with your other arm to create the sound of fist hitting face, and your partner should sharply turn their head in the direction of the punch.

The choke Place your hands around your partner's neck, but don't apply any pressure. Your partner grabs your wrists and controls all the action, throwing themselves from side to side, back and forth, while you follow their lead and fake the effort of choking.

The hair grab-and-throw When you grab your partner by the hair, he holds on to your wrist, and once again, it is he who controls the action, not you.

Kick to the groin Your partner stands with legs shoulder width apart. You aim a kick ostensibly at his nuts, but in fact the arch of your foot passes between his legs and only makes contact with his buttocks, providing a satisfying "thwok" sound. It's up to your partner to double over in ball-aching agony.

Kick to the stomach Your partner cups his hands together just in front of his stomach with the palms facing down, keeping his arms firm. Aim a kick at his hands. At the moment of impact, he doubles up in pain and jumps upward a little to give the illusion that the kick has lifted him briefly off the ground.

WET SNEEZE

Sometimes it's nice to let friends know just how much they mean to you. Dip your fingers into a glass of water and then sneeze violently when one of your friends walks by. Flick your wet fingers at them so that they get some spray on their face and think that you've just covered them with a few hundred thousand of your germs.

Tear a hole in a piece of paper and then tell someone that you are able to poke his or her entire body through the hole. This will lead them to believe that either you are about to lay an incredible shrinking head move on them (unlikely), or that somehow you are going to cut the paper in a clever way so that the size of the hole increases.

In fact you don't intend to do either of those things. All you need to do is stick your finger through the hole and then proceed to poke your hapless friend all over their body. There are few simpler ways of being this irritating!

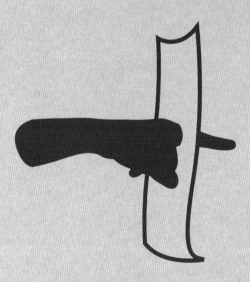

AUTO FINGER SLAP

It's a tall order getting someone to slap themselves against their will using their entire hand, but you can get them to slap themselves with one finger. Here's how.

Get your victim to splay their fingers and then place their palm on their nose so that the fingers fan out across their forehead. Now take their middle finger and try to pull it away from their face. Tell them that you are attempting a strength trick, and that they should resist your pulling with all their strength. Really fire them up by telling them that they will find it impossible to resist.

When you are sure that they have reached the maximum resistance, let go of their finger suddenly. It will snap back onto their forehead with a resounding "thwack!" and will probably sting a bit, as well as make them feel really stupid for being duped so easily.

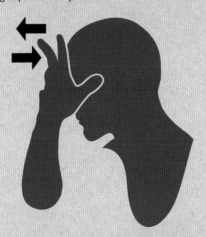

CHEEKY WATER DROP

When performed correctly, this trick produces the satisfying sound of a water droplet falling serenely in a dark cave. Done incorrectly, it sounds like breaking wind in a wet blanket.

Say the word "oil" and be aware of the shape your mouth and lips make when you make the "oi" sound. Exaggerate the shape of your lips—make them more round and then try to make an "oi" sound without vocalizing but by blowing air out of your mouth by bringing your tongue forward quickly, so that it ends up at the front of your mouth touching your lips (which are making an "oo" shape).

When you can make the "oi" sound consistently, it's time to transform the sound into a water droplet. This is done by flicking the side of the cheek with your finger at the same time you start to make the "oi" sound. It takes precision timing; if you get the two actions out of synch, it won't work, but when you do coordinate, the results speak for themselves. That was thirty hours well-spent!

CRACK AN EGG ON SOMEONE'S HEAD

Get your victim to sit in a chair. Show a hard-boiled egg to them, and then walk behind them so they can't see you hiding it in your pocket.

Next touch all four fingertips and the thumb tip of your left hand together and gently place the point where they meet on top of your victim's head. Using the palm of your right hand, hit the knuckle of your left hand smartly to produce a cracking sound (which will amplify nicely through the skull to reach their ears). Then create the feeling of runny yoke and white dripping down their scalp by opening the fingers of your left hand and brushing them lightly onto their hair as your "drip" the fingers of both hands down their head.

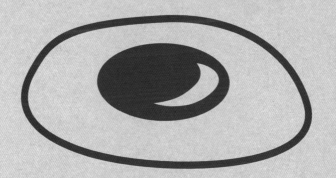

FOOT HYPNOTISM

Invite your subject to sit in a chair with both feet touching the ground. Get them to lift their right foot and rotate it at the ankle in a clockwise circle. As they continue to rotate their foot, announce that you are a foot hypnotist and you have the power to make them change the direction in which their foot is rotating and that they will be powerless to stop you. Explain that at no time during the trick will you touch them or interfere with their body.

Simply ask your subject to trace the number six in the air (the number not the word!) with the index finger of their right hand. This will make their foot change direction and start rotating counterclockwise. They may not even notice it at first, so you can have the great satisfaction of pointing out to them that their foot is totally under your control!

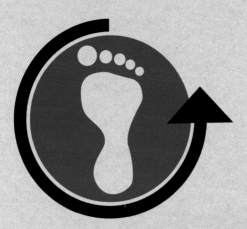

GLEEKING

Gleeking is a fancy and fascinating kind of spitting, only you do it by stimulating a gland located underneath your tongue. It's difficult to do, but once you've cracked the technique you'll be able to project a tiny jet of water several feet at will.

First you need to stimulate a yawn. For some people just thinking about yawning is enough to make it happen; if not, open your mouth wide and then think about yawning. That should do it. After yawning open your mouth in a loose "O" shape, push your bottom jaw out to create an overbite, while pressing down hard with the tip of your tongue on the fleshy bit just below your bottom front teeth. Open your mouth again as if to yawn and slowly lift and curl your tongue upward. Gleek!

If that doesn't work, here's another way that seems to work just as well. Suck air into your mouth below your tongue to stimulate the production of saliva, and then press your tongue tip to the roof of your mouth while bringing your lower jaw forward. Gleek!

These methods both rely on exerting pressure to the base of the tongue by pressing the tip against an area of the mouth, while simultaneously pushing the lower jaw forward. Play around with these two methods and you should be gleeking on the furniture in no time.

☆ LIGHTNING COIN GRAB ☆

Ask a friend to hold their palm at waist level, flat and face up, with a coin lying in the middle. How quickly do you think you can grab the coin? Quick enough so they don't have time to close their fingers to stop you? Try it now and see. Some of the time you might be lucky enough to grab it before they close their fingers, but nine times out of ten you'll probably fail.

Here's how to increase your hit rate to a near perfect score. The trick is to stop thinking consciously about grabbing the coin quickly, because the more you think about it, the greater the tension in your whole body and the easier it will be for your friend to notice when you make your move. The harder you try, the more you telegraph your intentions with your body. Instead, as you hold your hand above your friend's, try to imagine that the coin is already in your hand. When you have formed the image clearly in your mind, let your hand drop and take the coin.

You'll be amazed at the results. This visualization allows your subconscious mind to take over, which means that your body stays more relaxed and makes two things happen. You will take the coin quicker, and your friend's reactions will be slower because you will give them no clues.

Many martial arts utilize the technique of thinking beyond the target. If you want to break bricks with your hands (see page 10), you have to focus beyond the target. In this case the visualization makes you aim past the coin, so you hit your friend's hand with enough force so that the coin bounces into your hand.

TONGUE GUNSHOT

The next time you need to make the sound of a gunshot and you've left your gun at home, why not use your tongue?

This trick works best when you have some saliva in your mouth but your soft palate is dry. You need to create these conditions by biting your tongue a little to produce saliva, and then sucking air in through your teeth to dry out the soft palate.

Push the middle of the tongue tightly against the roof of your mouth just behind the top front teeth and then swallow hard to create a vacuum. Keeping the tongue tight against the top of the mouth, open your mouth and snap the tongue away to produce a loud gunshot sound.

If the noise is weak, then there was too much moisture in your mouth, your tongue was too wet, or you may be snapping the tongue away too slowly.

WIGGLE YOUR EARS

All of us possess muscles that will wiggle our ears, but not many people know how to flex them at will. Locating the muscles that control the ears is the first step in making them move. The auricularis superior fans out above the ear and the auricularis posterior is a smaller band of muscle that lies behind the ear.

Don't try to wiggle your ears; instead try to make your scalp tighten at the back of your jaw and across the back of your head. If you can do this, your ears will move too.

Place your fingers behind your ears and raise your eyebrows. If you feel the skin tightening at the back of your scalp, you are engaging the correct muscles to wiggle your ears. You may have experienced involuntary scalp tightening when you are cold and get a sudden scalp-shiver. You would probably see your ears wiggling slightly if you looked in the mirror at this precise moment.

Look in a mirror and stimulate the two muscles on both ears by massaging them gently with your finger. By stimulating the muscle in this way, you may be able to make yourself more aware of when it is tensing and relaxing. Look out for signs of movement, because your massaging may stimulate involuntary muscle movements.

If you do succeed in wiggling your ears, the movement will probably only be slight at first. If you practice, however, regularly to build up the muscle, you can increase the size of the ear wiggle, and perhaps even fan yourself at parties when you get too hot.

TWO POTATO

This stunt makes you look super strong and your victim will never figure out how you did it.

Ask your friend if they ever played "one potato, two potato, three potato, four" when they were a child. "Sure," they'll reply, demonstrating some fist on fist action to you. Bet them that no matter how hard they try to keep one fist (or potato) on top of the other fist, you will be able to separate them using just your index fingers. When they accept the challenge, you will triumph with ease (it's a leverage thing).

Now it's your turn, only instead of placing one fist on top of the other, you should wrap your upper fist around the thumb of your lower fist and grip hard. When your friend tries to pry your fists apart, they will fail, but they won't guess your secret. They will automatically assume that you are doing "one potato, two potato" because from the get go you used autosuggestion to put that image in their mind.

☆ CALORIC REFLEX TEST ☆

In medicine the caloric reflex test is used to test the vestibulo-ocular reflex. This reflex, if it is functioning properly, stabilizes images on the retina when the head is moved in one direction by making the eyes move in the opposite direction, much like an image stabilization system on a video camera.

However, it is possible to trigger this reflex by squirting water into the ear, because this stimulates the inner ear and nearby nerves. Here's what should happen:

* If you squirt cold water into the left ear, the eyes will turn quickly toward the right ear, and then slowly back.

* If you squirt cold water into the right ear, the eyes will turn quickly toward the left right ear, and then slowly back.

* If you squirt warm water into the left ear, the eyes will turn quickly toward the left ear, and then slowly back.

* If you squirt warm water into the right ear, the eyes will turn quickly toward the right ear, and then slowly back.

* If you put warm water in one ear and cold water in the other, the eyes will quiver back and forth, and the victim may feel disoriented and nauseous.

Make sure the water you use isn't at an extreme temperature. Cool or luke-warm water should still give good results.

COUGH THE PAIN AWAY

German scientists have discovered that if you cough (or sneeze) during an injection, it won't hurt as much. This is because a sudden cough or sneeze briefly raises the pressure in the chest and spinal fluid, which for a split second reduces the spinal cord's ability to transmit pain messages to the brain.

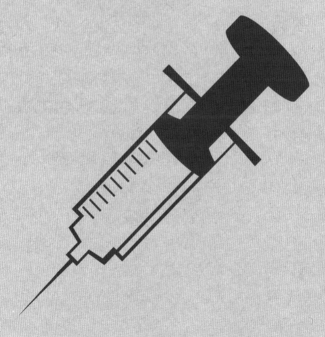

CURE AN ICE CREAM HEADACHE

An ice cream headache (also known as "brain freeze") is caused when the nerves in the roof of your mouth get so cold that blood vessels in the head dilate. Your body then overcompensates by suddenly trying to warm up your brain. You can reduce this effect by pressing hard against the roof of your mouth with the flat of your tongue. Another effective way of reducing the pain is to press an ice cube against your inner wrist.

CURE A TOOTHACHE

The next time you get a toothache, follow the advice of scientists in Canada who have discovered that if you rub an ice cube on the back of your hand, on the V-shaped area between your index finger and thumb, your pain will be reduced by as much as 50 percent. This is because the nerves in this area stimulate the brain to block pain signals from the hands and face.

DOORWAY SUPERHERO

This cheeky little trick gives the illusion that you are flying like a superhero. Next time you are in a room with a bunch of people, pretend to answer your cell phone, and then announce that something has come up and you have to save the world. As you leave you may even feel the need to remove your shirt to reveal the superhero T-shirt you are wearing underneath. Leave the door wide open as you go.

Take your position on the other side of the doorway, out of sight. Keeping your legs straight, bend your upper body at the waist so that it is horizontal, and extend your arms forward with the palms flat and facing the floor. Now walk forward slowly so that your fingers, arms, head, and upper torso appear in the doorway. If you keep your head in line with your arms and look down at the floor, it will give the impression that you are hundreds of feet up in the air. OK, no one is going to believe that you are really flying, but the trick's cheesiness is part of the reason why this hilarious stunt is so entertaining.

☆ FOREHEAD DRINKING ☆

Lie on the floor and balance a plastic or paper cup half-filled with water on your forehead. If you are reasonably fit and flexible, it is possible to drink the water without using your hands.

First you must bring your knees forward over your head, so that your knees reach your forehead. Use you hands to support your back if necessary. Next gently grip the cup between your knees and then bring your legs forward so that you can place the cup on the ground above your head. Finally pick up the cup with your teeth, tip your head back, and take a well-earned drink.

NEEDY KNEES

Who says you never give to charity? Here's a foolproof way to show that you are more than willing to give away large wads of your cash for needy causes.

The next time a tin rattler comes knocking at your door asking for money, invite them in and tell them you are going to fetch a hundred dollar bill. When you return, ask them to stand with their back to the wall with their heels touching the base board. Now place the hundred dollar bill on the floor about two feet in front of them. Tell them they can have the money; all they have to do is bend over and pick it up, without moving their feet or bending their knees.

HIPPY STRENGTH

It's easy to beat someone at a strength test if you know how to get them off-balance. Get your subject to stand facing you, with one of their arms straight out to the side, palm facing down. Now place two fingers on his wrist and push down and ask him to resist; he should be able to resist you with ease.

Now get him to stand with one foot standing on a hardback book (one that's at least an inch thick). When he tries to resist, you'll be able to push his arm down. This is possible because making him stand with one foot higher than the other subtly misaligns his hips. The brain recognizes that the spinal area is potentially vulnerable, and reduces the body's ability to resist in order to protect itself.

IMPOSSIBLE TIPTOES

Ask your victim if they can stand on their tiptoes. When they do, tell them that without touching them, you have the power to be able to stop them from standing that way.

Make them stand with their chin and waist pressed against the edge of an open door, with their feet on either side of the door. In this position, they find it impossible to lift their heels off the floor, let alone stand on tiptoes. This is because the door prevents them from shifting their center of gravity forward, which is necessary to lift the heels.

ONE LEG STAND

Ask your victim if they can balance on one leg. When they oblige, tell them that without touching them, you have the power to be able to stop them from balancing on one leg.

Make them stand against a wall with their right ear and right foot touching it. In this position they find it impossible to lift their left foot off the floor, let alone balance on the right. This is because the wall prevents them from shifting their center of gravity to the right, which is necessary to compensate for raising the left leg.

69

ROPE THROUGH FINGER

The effect of this trick is to wrap a piece of rope around your assistant's pinkie. Then you pull both ends of the rope and it passes clean through their finger.

You and your assistant (who is in on the trick) stand facing each other and sideways to the audience. Your assistant holds their right hand out, with palm facing toward the audience and with the fingers spread. You hang the middle of the rope over the pinkie so that both ends are dangling. First use your right hand to grip the rope end that is hanging down on your left, and then take the other end in your left hand. Your wrists should now be crossed. Uncross your hands so that the rope in your right hand passes in front of the rope on your left. Give a sharp pull on both ends. As long as your assistant keeps his fingers relaxed, the rope will slide off the finger as it bends and then the pinkie will spring back into position. It will happen so quickly that the rope will appear to pass through the pinkie.

Allow your audience to examine the rope so they can see that you're not using a trick one.

CLEAR YOUR SINUSES

When your nose is stuffed up, there's a natural way to clear your sinuses so that you don't have to resort to using nasal sprays and other nasty drugs.

Simply press between your eyebrows with one finger and then press your tongue against the roof of your mouth. Alternate for about thirty seconds and you'll feel your sinuses draining. This works because this action makes the vomer bone, one of the unpaired facial bones of the skull, rock back and forth, loosening congestion.

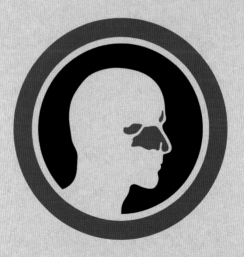

THUMB CONTROL

Take the thumb of your right hand and bend it so that the tip touches the middle of your palm on the same hand. Easy, isn't it? Your victim will find it hard to believe you when you announce that you have the power to stop them from being able to do this simple action, and that it will hurt when they attempt it.

Assure them that you won't use any props and that you won't touch them or harm them in any way. You won't even have to be in the same room as them to make it happen.

Instruct them to tuck the back of their hand into their armpit. Show them how to do it by doing it yourself, but don't touch them. Now walk out of the room and challenge them to try to touch thumb tip to palm. It's a very different story. Not only is it impossible, it's also painful to even attempt to move it because the tendons are already stretched to their limit.

★ BREAK A CONCRETE ★ BLOCK ON YOUR CHEST

Place three chairs in a row so that the distance between the end two chairs is the length of your body. Put on your protective eye goggles and lie down on the chairs with your head and shoulders at one end and your feet at the other.

Tense your body so that it can support itself, then get your assistant to remove the middle chair. Already you have created an illusion of super strength, although lying across two chairs is actually much easier than it appears.

Next ask your assistant to place a large concrete block on your chest (not on your stomach, because you won't be able to support its weight). If this wasn't impressive enough, get them to hit the block with a sledgehammer to split it in two. You would be surprised how easy this is, compared to how painful it appears. As long as the block is thick, it will absorb most of the energy from the sledgehammer, and by the time the energy reaches your body there will be too little left to do you any harm. After one or two hammer blows, the concrete block will split and you will appear superhuman!

CHAIR LIFT

Four people lifting one guy out of a chair using only their index fingers ought to be impossible, right? Well, actually it's not that hard. If an average guy weighs about 168 pounds, then each person only has to lift about 42 pounds. However, most people don't do the math and only focus on the idea that four fingers have to lift a grown man. You can make it appear that when they achieve this amazing feat is all due to your amazing powers of body manipulation and people management!

Begin the demonstration by getting your volunteer to sit in a chair. Tell him to relax (this will make him harder to lift), and then spend some time explaining how impossible it is to lift a guy with four fingers. The more you sow seeds of doubt into the four lifters, the less chance they have of making the lift. Then give them their first attempt. Ideally they will fail!

Tell them that they need to alter their mindset, combined with some nifty body magic, to make a successful lift. Get everyone to stack their palms one on top of the other on top of the volunteer's head (as if they were playing "one potato, two potato"). Tell the volunteer to tense his body and to resist the pressure (having a rigid body will make him easier to lift). Make them press down firmly for a count of twenty. Then they clasp their hands together with the index fingers sticking out straight and attempt the lift again. Two lift under the knees and two under the armpits.

This time they should be able to lift with ease for three reasons. You have programmed their minds to believe they can do it, the volunteer will feel much lighter when the downward pressure on his head has stopped, and his body will be rigid rather than limp making him much easier to lift.

FLOATING ARMS

Stand in a doorway with your hands by your sides and palms touching your thighs. Raise your arms up until the back of each hand is touching the doorframe. Using all your strength, push against the doorframe with each hand for about one minute, then walk away, relax your arms, and see where they go next.

FLOPPY FINGER

This is a trick that looks simple but can be hard to master until you really grasp how to position your finger correctly. The effect you create is that the bone has been removed from the tip of your pinkie.

Bend the pinkie of your dominant hand at the second joint (the one closest to your hand) so that it forms a right angle, with the tip parallel to the ground. Use your other hand to guide it into place if you find it too hard to do on its own. Keep the other fingers straight, and think about bringing the pinkie backward, which will help it to stay in place. Now flick the tip of your pinkie up and down, like you are plucking a guitar string. If your pinkie is in the right position and relaxed, the tip will flop up and down like a piece of rubber.

FROZEN HAND

This is another trick that relies on tiring out muscles in order to achieve the desired result. The effect is to freeze your victim's hand for several seconds so that they find it impossible to open it.

Get your volunteer to squeeze tightly on the fingers of your hand for about three minutes. Give them encouragement and try to make them squeeze even harder. Tell them that their hand is getting cold and hard like ice. When the three minutes are up, ask them to release their grip just enough for you to remove your hand. Then blow on their hand a few times and reinforce the idea that their hand is cold and hard. Announce that their hand is now frozen solid and that they won't be able to move it until it has thawed out. Enjoy watching them struggle for a few seconds while they try to unlock their fist.

POP YOUR EYEBALL WITH A FORK

Tricks with the eyes often have a high "euugh" factor, and this example has one of the highest. The effect is that you pierce your eyeball with a fork so that the juices squirt out.

To prepare for the trick, stick a large coin onto the back of an unopened creamer sachet with Blu Tack. This ensures that should you poke the fork too far, you don't end up poking your eye out for real.

Hold the fork in your dominant hand, and hide the creamer in your other hand, so that the coin is against your eye and the foil creamer lid is facing outward. After a few practice stabs to gauge the distance, make one decisive stab to puncture the creamer lid and squeeze your hand. The creamer will squirt white "eye milk" and make a sickening crunching sound. We leave how much screaming you do up to your discretion.

SEE IN THE DARK

There are much better ways of improving your night vision than eating carrots. Here are eight of them:

1. Protect your night vision. It takes thirty minutes for your eyes to adapt to near darkness, so avoid looking directly at bright objects.

2. Use your peripheral vision instead of looking directly at the object you want to see.

3. Keep your eyes moving to avoid fixating on one place, and thus adapting to the specific light conditions there.

4. Look for movement, contours, and shapes, rather than colors.

5. If you are using a light source such as a flashlight, use a dim bulb and place a red filter over it. This is especially useful when reading maps.

6. If you are exposed to light, keep one eye closed so that night vision is protected in that eye. Alternatively, wear an eye patch for protection.

7. Get lower than the object you want to view; this allows you to better make out its contours.

8. Squeeze your eyes tightly together for ten seconds then open them. It is thought that the resulting increased blood flow temporarily improves your night vision.

FOLDING EAR

This trick demonstrates how important our natural ear shape is to our ability to localize sound vertically. You'll need a set of keys to jangle.

Have your subject stand comfortably with their eyes closed. Stand directly in front of them and jangle your keys first at knee level (low), at waist height (middle), and then above their head (high). Explain what you are doing and where the keys are each time. Now pick one of these three positions at random, jangle your keys, and ask your subject to name the position: high, middle, or low. Repeat several times; someone with normal hearing should be able to name the position with ease.

Then ask them to fold over the top of each ear with a finger and repeat the experiment. Most people will find it impossible to correctly judge the position of the sound.

HEADLESS ON THE BEACH

This trick gives the illusion that you are lying on the sand with your head under your arm. You need three people and a beach towel.

This trick works best in soft sand that is a little bit damp but not compacted. Get two friends to bury you in the sand so that only your head is showing. You should be deep enough down so that there isn't a telltale lump in the sand that says, "Body buried here!"

The second person lies flat on their back on the sand with your head underneath their right arm. He covers his face with a beach towel and the third person covers his head with sand so that he looks like he's missing a head. The best way to do this is to make a hollow in the sand that the head can fit into so that it is lower than the rest of the body and wide enough for the person to breathe. The person who is lying down tilts his head to the side, so that when the sand is smoothed out it doesn't look like there's a head buried underneath.

Finally the third person sorts out the sand in the whole area so that it fits in with its surroundings. If the surrounding sand has wind patterns in it, then he will have to make some; if the surrounding sand is smooth, then he has to make it smooth. It should look as though you haven't disturbed the sand at all.

Try to coordinate your breathing with the rise and fall of the torso's chest and stomach, and maybe even attempt a coordinated sneeze or cough for maximum effect.

HEAVY AND LIGHT

Ask your subject to hold both arms out straight in front of their body with the palms flat and parallel to the ground. Make sure both arms are at the same level, then instruct them to close their eyes and keep their arms and hands fixed in the same place.

Tell them to imagine that a bag of groceries is being hooked over their right hand, and a bag of feathers over their left hand. Describe both objects to them in detail and stress the weight of one and the lightness of the other.

Soon you will see their right hand is considerably lower than the left, which rose up slightly while the other fell. Tell them to open their eyes; they will be surprised to see that their hands moved, even though they didn't feel it happening.

LEGS OF LEAD

Ask a volunteer to sit on the edge of a hard chair, with their bottom at the front and their feet flat on the floor, thighs parallel to the ground. Challenge them to lift their knees up and keep them in the air for three seconds. They will find this impossible because their center of gravity is too far forward to allow them to lift their feet. Make sure you ask them to lift their knees rather than their feet, because it is possible to move the feet by sliding them forward and then up. Highlighting the knees avoids this opportunity.

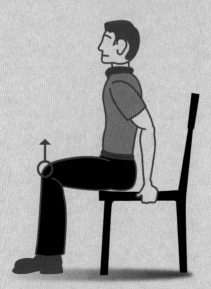

Everyone knows that if you bend one of your fingers in the middle it looks like half of it is missing; you're never going to fool anyone by doing that on its own. However, this variation of the trick relies on speed and misdirection to fool the viewer into having a disconcertingly real experience of digit amputation.

Begin with both your hands flat, with the fingers closed and the palms facing your body at head height. Show your hands to the audience, then keeping your hands flat, place your left hand over your right fingertips, and touch your left thumb to the middle fingertip on your right hand. With the thumb and middle finger still touching, hinge your left hand out of the way, then back into position again.

Now use your left hand to make it look as though you are twisting and pulling something. Bend the middle finger of your right hand in the middle, and then slide your left hand away to reveal the missing fingertip. Of course this on its own would have no effect, since everyone would know you were simply bending your finger out of sight. What comes next makes all the difference, and you have to practice so you can do it cleanly and at great speed.

A split second after you reveal the missing fingertip, turn your right hand 180 degrees so that the palm faces outward, straighten your middle finger, close the index and middle finger together, and the third and pinkie together, leaving a gap between (i.e., the Vulcan "Live long and prosper" sign). Then immediately flip your hand back to the first position and slide your left hand back over it again to "replace" the missing fingertips. Straighten your now concealed middle finger, and slide the left hand away to reveal the intact right hand digits.

If you perform this section of the stunt really fast, it tricks the eye of the viewer into thinking that your middle finger wasn't bent but removed, since you show them the backs of your fingers.

MOONWALK

The peculiar art of gliding backward while apparently walking forward was made famous by Michael Jackson during the 1980s. It's actually a lot easier than you might think.

When they try to do the moonwalk, most people wrongly bend their knee, place their toe tip on the ground, and move the leg backward. That's not going to work. Instead, you need to lift your right heel, keeping your left leg straight and left foot flat on the ground. Most of your body weight should be on your right toes, so that you can slide your left foot backward, keeping your left leg straight and foot flat on the ground.

After completing that first step, it's time to move your right leg. Lift your left heel, bend your left leg at the knee, and transfer your body weight onto the toes of your left foot. At the same time straighten your right leg, lower your right heel, and slide your right foot back, keeping it flat on the ground. And repeat!

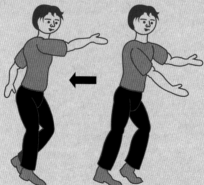

For this trick you'll need a couple of those little round nonslip rubber gripping pads you can buy cheaply from hardware stores.

Place the gripping pad on the table and the jar on top. Twist the lid. If the lid isn't too tight, it should come off easily, and the pad will stop the jar from twisting. If you're opening the jar for the first time, you probably need to use the next method.

Place a gripping pad in the crook of your elbow (or even your armpit), place the jar on top, followed by another gripping pad. Clamp the jar tightly in your elbow/armpit (making sure it is vertical, so the contents don't spill out) and use your hand to twist off the lid. Easy!

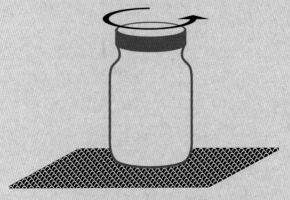

PHANTOM BALL

Place your hands on either side of an imaginary soccer ball and hold it out on front of you. Invite your subject to place their hands over yours and tell them to press firmly into the imaginary ball to squash it inward. Match their inward force by pressing outward with your hands, so that all your hands remain in the same position. Ask your subject to gradually increase the pressure, and you match it.

After a minute ask your subject to close their eyes and gradually reduce the pressure; as the pressure reduces move your hands away and tell them it's their turn to hold the ball.

For a few seconds they will now feel a phantom ball they can squeeze and manipulate between their hands.

PIERCE YOUR EAR WITH YOUR THUMB

This trick gives a very credible impression that you are able to push your thumb through the skin at the back of your earlobe. The skill in execution lies with a combination of manual dexterity and acting your socks off. Piercing your ear is uncomfortable to say the least, so make the pain look convincing, and even throw in a little fake blood when you've perfected the finger moves.

First show your right ear to the audience. Grab the earlobe and flick it a few times to show that nothing is concealed in it and that it's really your ear. Don't tug on it at this stage or you might unwittingly telegraph the trick to your audience.

Now turn your head away from the audience briefly, and holding the back of your right hand flat against the side of your head, grip the top of the ear between your index finger and thumb. Rotate your hand clockwise until you can grip the earlobe at the bottom of the ear with your index finger. If you want to add blood, now's the time: Use your left hand (which has fake blood on the fingertips) to hold your right ear to help give you apparent leverage as you pretend to force your thumb even further through the skin. When you remove your left hand, the blood will be visible on both hands. What a messy business.

The skin of your upper ear should now be curled around your thumb, and the earlobe at the bottom should curl around your thumb from the other direction. The place where these parts meet will be concealed by your fist, and it appears as if your thumb has passed through your ear.

Pull your finger and thumb away from your head slightly, giving the audience a better view of the hole that you've made. Pull your fingers away and bring your hand back, allowing the ear to spring back into place. Let the audience examine your ear to show that it is intact again.

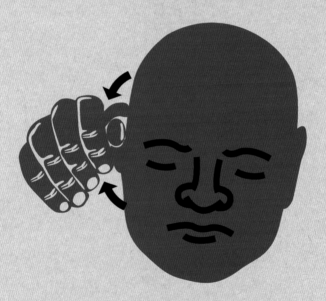

RING FINGER GLUED TO THE TABLE

Place your palm flat on the table with the fingers splayed. Get your victim to do the same. Then ask them to lift their fingers off the table, without raising the palm, which they will do with ease.

Tell them that you have the power to stop them from moving their ring finger without touching it. Bend their middle finger so that it is tucked into the palm. When they attempt to lift the ring finger, while keeping their palm on the table, it will be stuck!

SUPPORT THE WEIGHT OF TEN PEOPLE

This wonderful little stunt will fool anyone who isn't a civil engineer into thinking that you are as hard as nails and can withstand the weight of ten people (or as many more as you have available—there's no limit to how many people you can take on).

Stand with your legs shoulder width apart facing a wall. Stretch your arms straight out in front of you and then lean forward until your hands are resting flat against the wall. Your body should be leaning at about 40 degrees from the vertical.

Now get the first person to adopt the same position as you, only instead of leaning their hands against the wall, they use the back of your shoulders for support. The third person leans on the shoulders of the second person, and so on.

It doesn't matter how many people you add to the chain, the only weight you'll actually have to support is that of the person directly behind you because each person's weight is directed through the legs of the person in front of them. However, to an observer it looks as though you are taking the weight of the world on your shoulders.

TIE A SHOELACE WITH ONE HAND

Here's how to tie the shoelaces of your right shoe. To do the left shoe, simply reverse some of the directions.

First cross one shoelace over the other, and then bring one end behind the other to form a simple overhand knot. Pull the left end of the lace to the left and trap it underneath your left shoe. Next, keeping your left shoe on the left lace end, pull the right lace end to the right and wiggle your right foot to the right until the knot is tight. Tuck that same lace into the tongue of your shoe to make a loop. Wrap the inside lace around that loop and back through itself to form the second loop. Finally pull both loops tight using your thumb, index, and middle fingers.

HAND CONTROL

This stunt gives the illusion that you are controlling someone's hand against their will, when you are actually misdirecting the audience into misinterpreting what is really going on.

Get your subject to sit on a chair behind a small table that is covered with a tablecloth reaching down to the ground (so nobody can see underneath the table). Ask your subject to place their hand flat on the table in front of them. Sit down at the table so that you are sideways to them.

Place your hand on their hand and place your foot on their foot (out of sight of the audience). Pretend that you are pressing on their hand, but simultaneously press their foot gently with your foot. Ask them if they can feel the pressure. They will reply that they can. At this point the audience believes that the subject is referring to hand pressure.

Instruct your subject that you would like them to close their eyes and raise their hand the next time they feel the same pressure. Pretend to be mentally willing their hand to feel pressure, even though your hand is nowhere near theirs. When you are sure that you have formed a mental connection with their hand, press their foot firmly. This is the subject's signal to raise their hand, but the audience will think you hypnotized them or used telekinesis.

HANDY STRING

This stunt uses the power of suggestion and works best on people who have a receptive imagination (i.e., children). It works on adults about 30 percent of the time.

Ask your subject to stand facing you with their hands pressed flat together in front of them about a foot away from their body with the fingers pointing toward you. Rub your own palms and fingers together very fast to create some heat. Then wiggle your fingers up and down vertically on either side of their hands, as close as you can without touching them. This should create a lot of air movement, and your subject should feel a slight breeze as you whoosh your fingers up and down for about fifteen seconds.

Now move your hands so that one is above and one is below the subject's hands. Repeat the whooshing, only this time from side to side. Quickly pinch some imaginary skin on either side of their hands and pretend to draw a piece of string out from either side of their hands for a few inches. Holding the string tautly between fingers and thumbs, move it back and forth within their palm, up and down, and forward and back.

If you can really imagine the string fully and perform the mime with conviction, your suggestible subject will experience the eerie sensation of string moving around inside their palms.

⭐ TOUCHING FINGERTIPS ⭐

It is relatively easy to touch your index fingers together from a starting position of an arm's width apart, as long as you do it slowly. The quicker you go, the harder it becomes. This trick exploits this fact by putting subtle pressure on the victim to speed up without realizing it.

First demonstrate what you want your victim to do. Stand with your arms as wide apart as they will go and stick out your index fingers. Stay relaxed and bring your fingers smoothly together until the tips touch in front of your chest. Easy.

Now it's your victim's turn. It is important that you stress how difficult this is to immediately put doubt into their mind. Next tell them to limber up a bit so that they can really focus on getting it right. Ask them to perform a couple of jumping jacks or run in place for fifteen seconds, all in the name of mental and physical preparation. In fact what you are doing is raising their heart rate and preparing them to perform the challenge much faster than you did. When you are satisfied that your victim is in a peak state of arousal, shout "GO!" and lunge toward them. They will feel under pressure, and this, combined with the physical exertion, will make them go too fast with spectacularly poor results!

TWISTED WRIST

In this trick you appear to twist someone's arm further than it should be able to go without causing them unimaginable pain!

Before you begin hide a plastic cup inside your clothes underneath your armpit, so that you can simulate the crunching of bones by squeezing your arm against your side while performing the trick.

Your subject stands sideways to you and extends their arm with the palm loosely open and facing the sky. Using your right hand, place your fingers on the inside of their wrist and your thumb on the top of the wrist. Tap the crook of their elbow with your left hand; this will encourage them to allow you to bend their arm at the elbow, so that the forearm is vertical. As you do this, twist the hand counterclockwise so that their fingertips are pointing to the side of their head (as if they were going to brush something off their shoulder).

Now twist their hand in a smooth and swift clockwise motion around 180 degrees, so that the fingers point at you. Squeeze the plastic cup in your armpit for the last 45 degrees to make the sound of crunching tendons. Then take hold of their hand in a handshake and bring their arm down, while turning the hand back again. It will look as if their hand completed a full rotation.

360-DEGREE TONGUE TWISTER

If you can rotate your tongue, you can do this trick. First rotate your tongue as far as it will go in a clockwise direction. Hold it there and close your mouth over your tongue so just the tip shows through. Now rotate the tongue counterclockwise as far as it will go. As long as you keep your tongue tip in view, it will look as if you have performed the impossible by rotating your tongue 360 degrees!

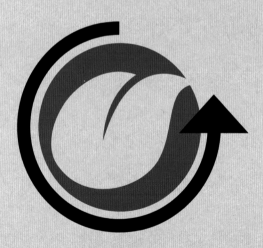

☆ AUTO CANNIBALISM ☆

When you're feeling hungry, why not chow down on one of your fingers? It's free meat and you know where it came from better than anyone!

Splay your fingers and present the back of your hand to the audience, then single out your index finger and wiggle it a few times. Now pop it into your mouth just up to the second joint, suck on it, and remove. Lick your lips with relish. Repeat a couple of times. This is the calm before the horror!

The next time you pop your finger into your mouth, tuck it into your palm so that you end up only sucking the second joint. Practice in front of a mirror until you can get the positioning right so that it looks like your whole finger is in your mouth.

Now put some effort into chewing through the tendons, tissue, and bone-joint of your finger. If you've ever eaten a chicken leg, you'll know what this feels like. Bare your teeth (keep them closed) and rotate your finger back and forth a little as you chew, then pull the hand away as if ripping away the very last bit of stubborn skin.

To replace the fingertip, grab your finger with the fist of your other hand and then slide the fist along the finger to reveal its full length restored.

BREAKDANCE

Here are two basic breakdancing moves: the Kick-up and the Windmill. If you learn just these two and put them together in a combo, a few people may be fooled into thinking you can breakdance. Life's too short to learn for real, right?

Kick-up Sit on the ground with your legs in front of you, bent at the knees. Roll back, place your hands on the ground on either side of your head, bend your elbow, and support your weight with your fingers, which are pointing away from the head, and the thumbs are pointing to your feet. Bring your legs right back over your head and then kick your legs forward and up, and then bring your feet under when you land on your toes. Kick back again so your upper body lands back on the floor, with your shoulder blades and hands taking the rolling contact with the floor. Keep up the momentum and kick your legs forward, up, and under again, and so on.

The Windmill Lie flat on your back in a star shape with legs and arms straight and wide open. Rotate your legs around a vertical axis while also rotating your upper body around a horizontal axis. Keep your legs wide open to give you momentum. After one full upper body rotation, place your right hand flat on the ground in front of your waist and lock it into the lower stomach and roll onto your right elbow. Keep spinning with your lower body to create a turntable spin.

CHOP THROUGH YOUR WRIST

First remove any wrist adornments such as a watch or bracelet. Hold your bare left arm in front of you just below chest level, with the hand flat and the palm facing your right elbow.

Form your right hand into a rigid "karate chop" position and make a few practice taps on the wrist of your left hand, so that the first joint of the pinkie of your right hand makes contact with the middle of the left wrist.

On the third chop relax your right hand and bring your left arm up slightly, so that when you make the strike the fingers of your right hand will bend around the left wrist. At the end of the movement, make your right hand rigid again. It will look as though your hand passed through your wrist.

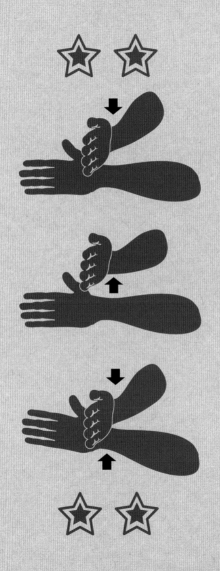

DOUBLE LEG DISAPPEARANCE

Make both your legs disappear behind a towel—first the right, then the left, then both of them together.

This trick doesn't really stand up to careful scrutiny, so only do it once, otherwise your audience may figure it out. First explain to your audience what you are about to do. This trick really only works if your audience is slightly higher than you so that their sight line underneath your legs is slightly restricted. You don't want anyone to see directly underneath your legs and beyond. A good position is to make your audience stand on the second step of a staircase, and you perform the trick at the bottom of the steps.

Place the towel in front of you so that it completely hides your lower body. Then lift the towel up twelve inches to reveal both your feet still on the floor. Then stand on your left leg and bend the right leg behind you. Lift up the towel twelve inches to show that your right leg has vanished. Quickly lower the towel and place your right foot back down exactly where it was before, and lift up your left leg. Raise the towel twelve inches to show that your left leg has vanished. Quickly lower the towel again, only this time place your left leg on the floor about a foot further back than it was before.

Finally transfer your weight to your left leg and raise your right leg out of sight. Because your audience has become accustomed to seeing your feet in a particular place, when you quickly lift the towel up and down again to give your audience a glimpse of thin air they won't realize that you have merely moved your left foot back out of sight. They will think that both legs have vanished!

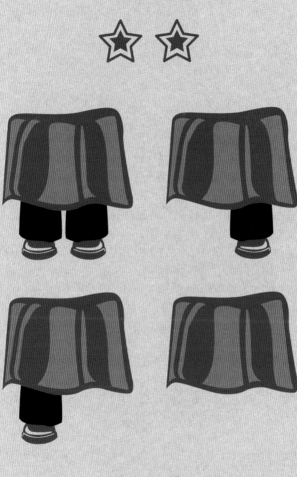

GLUED EYELIDS

This stunt gives the appearance to an audience that you can hypno-tize a person such that they find it impossible to open their eyes.

Stand facing your volunteer; tell them to relax and take a few deep breaths. Explain that you are going to hypnotize them in order to temporarily glue their eyelids shut. Tell them to stay relaxed and that at no point will they experience any pain or any real glue!

Hold your index finger it front of their face, about a foot away, and get your subject to focus intently at it. Move your hand from side to side, and make sure that their eyes follow your finger as it moves. Explain that this is part of the hypnotism and that their eyelids may at this point start to feel a bit heavy. After about twenty seconds bring your finger to a halt in the middle, confirm that they are still focusing on the fingertip, and then bring your finger forward until it touches the top of their forehead. Ask them to close their eyes while keeping their focus fixed on the tip of your finger.

Now get your subject to visualize your finger on an imaginary screen at the top of their forehead, and, while they maintain this focus, to try to open their eyes. They won't be able to because no one can open their eyes when their eyeballs are straining upward as far as they can go. However, your audience will believe that you have used the power of hypnotism to glue their eyes shut.

To release them from your apparent spell, bring your finger down their forehead onto the tip of their nose, then remove your finger and ask them to open their eyes after a count of three.

HEADSTAND

This trick makes your victim think that you are able to place your leg on the top of their head. It works best on someone who is much taller than you and when there are only two of you in the room.

Explain what you intend to do, and say that you will succeed because of your amazing flexibility and self-belief! Begin the trick by pointing both your index fingers at your victim's eye level. Bring your fingers slowly toward their eyes and tell them to focus on your fingers. When your fingers are about two inches away from their face, ask them to close their eyes, at which point you place the index and middle finger of your right hand gently on their forehead just above the eyes. Don't put your fingers on their eyes, because if they react suddenly you could cause a nasty injury.

Because the last things your victim saw were your two hands approaching, they will assume that both your hands are on their forehead. They will get a big surprise when you place your left arm heavily on top of their head (which you tell them is your leg). Then remove your arm, take your fingers away from their forehead, and tell them to open their eyes.

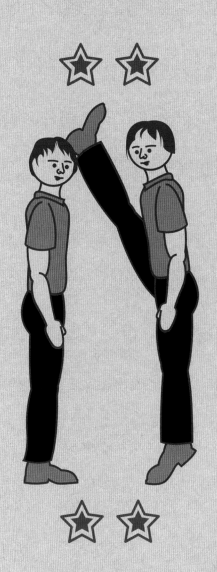

STOP HICCUPS

There are literally dozens of theories on the best way to stop the hiccups, and none of them are guaranteed to work for everyone. Here are ten ways to try. If you're desperate, just cycle through them until one of them works.

1. A spoonful of sugar. Take a large spoonful of sugar and shove the whole thing in your mouth at once. If you can get it on the back of the tongue—without choking—this works best. And kids love it.

2. Boo! A good startle can shock the hiccups right out of someone. Be careful not to accidentally hit the victim, though, or surprise them so much they hit you.

3. Drink up. Fill a regular water glass all the way to the top. Then drink the whole thing down without stopping—or until you can't take any more.

4. Bend over and drink up. Pour yourself a glass of water and put it on the floor next to your feet. Then stand up and bend over as far as you can. Staying in this position, drink as much of the water as you can.

5. Bag it. Get a paper lunch sack and form a bottleneck at the top with your hands. Put it over your mouth and breathe in and out until the hiccups go away. Stop before you pass out.

6. Plug your ears. Stick your fingers in your ears and press gently. Be careful not to press too hard or put your fingers too far in. Keep up the pressure until the hiccups stop.

7. Hold your breath. Take a big gulp of air and hold it. Then bear down on your diaphragm. Hold your breath as long as you can. If you hiccup in the middle of this, just start over until it works.

8. Try an antacid. Take an over-the-counter kind. The medication can help settle the irritation causing the hiccups.

9. Bribe them. To stop someone else's hiccups, tell them, "I'll give you twenty bucks if you can hiccup again!"

10. Wait. Most hiccups go away all by themselves in less than a half an hour. If you have hiccups for more than an hour, it might be time to call a doctor.

IMPROVE YOUR VISION WITH YOUR FIST

People without perfect vision can't always have their corrective lenses with them. Maybe you lost your contact lenses. Or maybe it's just first thing in the morning and you want to be able to read your alarm clock without putting your glasses on. If you ever find yourself in such a fix, try this.

Make a fist with either hand. Leave a small hole through the middle of it, about the thickness of a drinking straw.

Peer through the hole at something that looks blurry. Squeeze your fist slightly, letting only a tiny shaft of light eke its way through.

The image in your fist should get sharper. It may not entirely correct for your nearsightedness, but it should be noticeable—and maybe enough for you to be able to read that alarm clock.

CATCH QUARTERS OFF YOUR ELBOW

Those of us old enough to have watched Happy Days *remember this trick from the TV show. To pull it off, just follow these directions and practice.*

1. Raise your arm (use the one attached to your favored hand) and bend back your elbow so that your upper arm is parallel to the floor.

2. Bring your hand around so that your palm faces the ceiling, and cup your fingers.

3. Place a coin (a quarter works well here) on your upper arm near your elbow.

4. In one smooth motion, bring your arm forward.

If you do this right, the coin should slip off your elbow and wind up in your hand. All you have to do is close your hand around the coin, and you should be able to catch it easily.

Once you master catching a single coin, try this trick with larger and larger stacks of coins. Then challenge your friends to see who can catch the most.

STIFLE A SNEEZE

Most of the time, if you have to sneeze, you should just find yourself a tissue and let it rip. Your body sneezes to get rid of something inside that's irritating. Sometimes, though, you need to put a stop to it, at least for a moment. If so, here are ten different tricks to try.

1. Press your teeth. Push the tip of your tongue as hard as you can against your two front teeth where they meet the top of your mouth.

2. Blow your nose. Find a tissue and blow your nose softly. This may get rid of whatever is inside of you that makes you need to sneeze.

3. Press your lip. As funny as it looks in the cartoons, pressing a finger against your upper lip can actually work. Apply firm but not painful pressure on your lip, right where the lip meets the bottom of your nose.

4. Pinch yourself. Find a sensitive part of your body and give it a little pinch. Some people recommend the skin between your index finger and thumb.

5. Bite your lip. Suck the inside of your upper lip between your teeth and press down on it with your teeth. Be careful not to bite too hard.

6. Tickle your palate. Use the tip of your tongue to tickle the top of your mouth. Focus on the area where the hard and soft palates meet.

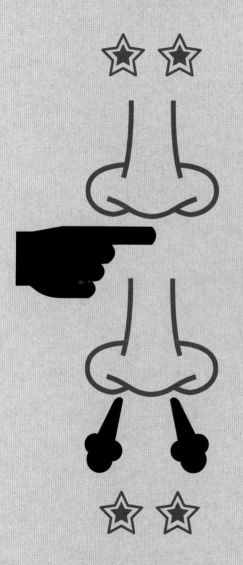

121

7. Pinch your nose. Use your index finger and thumb to pinch the bridge of your nose and press in toward your eyes. If it doesn't work, at least you've already covered your mouth.

8. Hold your breath. Take a deep breath and hold it for as long as you can. Bearing down on your diaphragm also helps.

9. Massage your lobe. Reach up and grab an earlobe between your index finger and thumb. Wiggle it back and forth.

10. Think it away. Focus intensely on something else. This can be a blank spot on the wall, your navel, or anything handy. Stare at it until the need to sneeze goes away.

CRUSH A CAN ON YOUR FOREHEAD

If you want to impress your friends with what a hardcore party animal you are, when you finish your next canned drink, smash it flat against your forehead. Then toss it in the nearest recycling bin. Tell them you made an effort to reduce the can's volume because of your undying interest in doing whatever it takes to preserve the environment.

If you do this wrong, you can end up with a circular bruise on your forehead, so be careful. Try practicing at home first.

1. Pick the right kind of can. Aluminum soda and beer cans work best. Avoid cans for energy drinks and the like that have a sealed rim on the bottom as well as the top.

2. Put the palm of your hand on top of the can. Lower your fingers and thumb around the shaft of the can.

3. Squeeze the shaft of the can and make little dents in it. If you can't do this, put the can down and walk away.

4. Raise the can in front of your face and line it up with your forehead.

5. Bring your head forward and shove the can into your forehead with one sharp movement. As you do this squeeze the can with your thumb and fingers, crushing its shaft. Take care not to smash yourself in the nose or eyes, and watch those fingers. If the can crushes onto them too fast, you could get cut or pinched.

6. Show the can to your astonished friends and dispose of it properly.

If you don't crush the shaft of the can before you smash it into your head, you will wind up with a headache. To practice you can do this in slow motion. Crush the can as you press it firmly against your forehead and you will see how it works.

☆ REMOVE YOUR THUMB ☆

With a little practice—and a bit of distance from your witnesses—you can make it look like you can pull your thumb right off your hand.

1. Make fists with your hands. With your right hand tuck your thumb inside your fingers. With your left wrap your first two fingers around your thumb and let the tip of your thumb stick out between your ring and middle fingers.

2. Stack your left fist on top of your right fist with the hands reversed so that the fingers of your right hand face toward you and the fingers of your left hand face away. Fit the butt of one thumb flush up against the other. Your elbows should stick straight out from each other. If you do this right, your left thumb will look like it's attached to your right hand.

3. Separate your stacked fists and then put them right back together. With a smooth enough move, it will look like you pulled off your thumb and put it right back on.

FIND YOUR BLIND SPOT

In each one of your eyes, there's a spot where the optic nerve attaches to the back of your retina. Your retina cannot see the light that hits this spot, but your brain fills in the missing area with information from your other eye, so you normally don't notice it. To find it, try this.

1. On a piece of paper, draw a small back dot about the size of a pencil's eraser. About an inch to the right of this, write the numbers 1 to 9. Leave a little space between each of them.

2. Lean over the paper with your face five or six inches away from it. Cover your right eye and look at the black dot. Then slowly move your head to the right over each of the numbers in order, keeping your vision focused straight down. As you do this watch the black dot out of the corner of your eye.

3. At some point the black dot will vanish. That's because it's in your blind spot.

You can do the same thing with your right eye by writing the numbers to the left of the dot and covering your left eye.

Try this with different colors of paper. When the dot disappears, your brain automatically fills in the blind spot with the surrounding color.

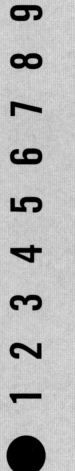

FART WITH YOUR HANDS

With a little practice, you can make the sounds of flatulence with your hands. If you can't figure this one out, ask any middle-school kid for help. Quietly.

1. Hold your hands up with your fingers together and your thumbs apart, as if you're wearing a pair of mittens.

2. Cup your hands and then clasp them together. The fingers of your right hand should sit between the thumb and index finger of your left hand (or vice versa). Leave a little space between your palms, as if you had a ping-pong ball between them.

3. Make a good seal around the air pocket between your palms. Then squeeze your hands together. You should feel the resistance of the air trying to escape.

4. Keep squeezing until the air escapes. The noise it makes as it leaves sounds like a fart.

Some people find it easier to cup a hand under an armpit to produce the same effect. You just crank your upper arm up and down over the cupped hand.

BLOW A TWO-FINGER WHISTLE

The next time you want to hail a taxi or stop every bit of conversation in a room, just break out the two-finger whistle. With practice you can make this much louder than a regular whistle and get the attention you need when you need it.

1. Hold your index finger and thumb together in a circle, just like you're making the OK sign.

2. Roll both of your lips back over your teeth.

3. Put your index finger and thumb inside your mouth, touch your tongue to the spot where your finger and thumb touch, and blow. Use short, sharp exhalations and fiddle around.

Keep practicing until you get it right. However, don't do it for too long in any single sitting, or you could get dizzy or even pass out.

STICK OUT YOUR TONGUE AND TOUCH YOUR NOSE

Unless you're Gene Simmons, you probably can't stick out your tongue like a tentacle and smack it on the tip of your nose. However, with a little practice, you should be able to manage just barely touching it.

1. Stick your tongue out as far as you can. Stretch it for a few seconds and bring it to a point.

2. Bring your upper lip down to cover your teeth.

3. Use your lower lip to help push your tongue up over your upper lip until you touch the base of your nose. It helps if you relax—tension can cause your tongue to shorten instead of stretch.

If you're a smart aleck, there's an easier way to "stick out your tongue and touch your nose."

1. Stick out your tongue.

2. Stick out your index finger and use it to touch your nose.

HOW TO TAKE A PUNCH

Houdini used to challenge people to hit him in the stomach as hard as they could. With the right kind of preparation and practice, you should be able to pull off the same trick. Just make sure you're ready for it before the guy starts to swing or you'll go down like a cheap pillow.

1. Get into shape. If you have abs of pudding, there's no way you're going to be able to take a solid punch. The padding from your spare tire might absorb some of the blow, but the rest of it will likely knock you silly. Try lots of crunches to build up those abdominal muscles.

2. Brace yourself. Plant your feet solidly on the ground, about as far apart as your shoulders. This may not help you take the punch, but should help keep you from getting knocked over.

3. Tighten your abs. Flex your abdominal muscles until they're as tight as you can make them. This is your best defense.

4. Exhale. When the punch comes at you, blow out hard. This helps tighten your abs even more. Also, you can't get the wind knocked out of you if you blow it out first.

5. Grunt when you're hit. This helps you remember to exhale, and it adds a bit of drama to the process.

6. Grin and bear it. The punch will hurt, no matter how ready you may be. Man up and take it with a smile.

DO A BACKFLIP

This bit of gymnastic trickery is both flashy and dangerous. There's a reason so few people attempt it. If you mess it up, you could maim or kill yourself. If you pull it off, though, you'll impress everyone around.

1. Line up some trained spotters and a gymnastic mat. In a pinch a futon or a mattress may do. Your spotters should be strong enough to catch you. Don't try this with your kid sister. Stick with this until you're very, *very* good at it.

2. Wear loose clothes and decent athletic shoes. You don't need your equipment working against you.

3. Relax. Get yourself in a confident frame of mind. There's no chickening out once you start. Trying to stop yourself mid-flip can really get you hurt.

4. Put your feet together and let your arms hang down at your side.

5. Dig down by bending your knees no more than 90 degrees.

6. Swing your arms backward.

7. Swing your arms forward as you jump as high as you can straight up in the air.

8. When you reach the top of your jump, roll backward and tuck in your legs. Bring your arms forward to your knees and pull on them to help with your momentum.

9. Unroll your back as you prepare to land, but keep your knees partially bent. Try to land flat on your feet to keep yourself from falling over.

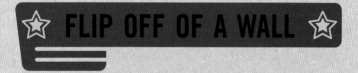

FLIP OFF OF A WALL

Ever seen an action film in which a character runs up to a wall, walks up it, and flips over backward? It's insanely dangerous but looks great, which is why they put it in the film.

1. Think safety first. Line up some spotters (ones who know what they're doing) and place a mattress, futon, or other padding below your landing spot. Twisting an ankle or cracking your wrist might suck, but breaking your neck will ruin your whole day. Also, learn how to do a back flip first (see page 134). That skill set is essential for this trick.

2. Find a good wall. You need something that's solid and uniform. You also need a surface where your shoes can get a good grip. Bare brick works best.

3. Set up your spotters and mattress. (So, that's safety both first and third.)

4. Run straight at the wall. Don't sprint, just hold a steady, reasonable pace. As you run pick out the spot where you're going to plant your foot on your second step up the wall. This should be about as high as your chest.

5. Plant your off-foot first. This is usually on the same side as your off-hand, so if you're a righty, lead with your left foot. Push yourself up the wall as if you're running up a very steep hill.

136

6. Plant your second foot at chest level and keep pushing yourself up the wall. As you go higher lean back and bring up your off-foot as if you were still running up the wall. This helps give you the momentum you need to flip your body around.

7. Once you are horizontal, crane your neck back. Look at the ground and pick a spot for your landing. Keep your eyes on the spot, and tuck your legs around and under you. Keep your knees bent but not too tightly. You'll need some space to absorb the impact of the landing.

8. Land on your feet.

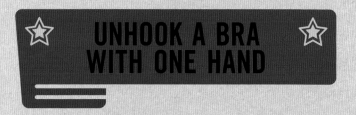

UNHOOK A BRA WITH ONE HAND

A bra can be a difficult contraption to figure out—whether you're the woman wearing it or the man trying to help a woman out—but this trick will teach you how to easily maneuver the often pesky clasp with just one hand. After a little practice, you'll be a pro in no time.

1. Make sure you are dealing with the right kind of bra. Some models clasp in the front and others have multiple sets of hooks in the back. Ideally, you want to work with one that has clasps in the rear with just a pair of hooks.

2. Regardless of if you're a woman or a man, reach around with your designated hand and lift up the back of the shirt that is covering the bra.

3. Find the clasp with your hand. If you're female, you know where this is. If you're male, it should be somewhere near the center of the woman's back along her spine.

4. A standard bra's clasp has bent hooks that fit inside small metal loops. Locate the side with the loops on it and push down on this with your middle finger.

5. Reach over with your index finger and thumb and grasp the other side of the clasp.

6. Pinch the two sides together and lift the side with the hooks up a little. It should come free.

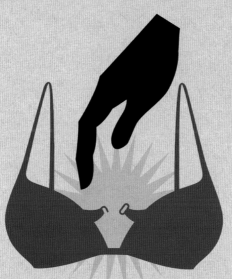

ELEVEN FINGERS

Here's a neat way of fooling someone into believing you've got eleven fingers, or at least tricking them into wasting a few moments of their life paying attention to the absurd logic of your flawed argument.

Point to each digit on your left hand with your right index finger, and count: "one, two, three, four, five."

Then use your left index finger to count the digits on your right hand: "six, seven, eight, nine, ten."

"That's weird," you say, in bemusement, "I must have missed one! I'll have another try."

This time, start counting backwards on the digits of your left hand: "Ten, nine, eight, seven, six."

Stop and hold up your right hand and say: "and five makes eleven!"

TWISTED WRIST

Getting rapped on the knuckles is no fun, but doing it to yourself is for crazy people. Here's how to fake a knuckle rap and appear immune to pain. It's a great trick to do when you've had too much to drink and your friends are calling you a chicken because you won't accompany them to the tattoo parlor.

Tap your knuckles a few times against the edge of a table, and widen your eyes to suggest that you relish self-inflicted pain. On the final swing, bring your arm down really fast and open your fist briefly so that your fingertips strike the edge of the table as your hand slaps downward, and then make a fist again immediately, so that it looks like your knuckles took the full force of the impact. The woody crack and your slightly deranged grin will put to rest any niggling doubts in the assembled company about your ability to withstand pain!

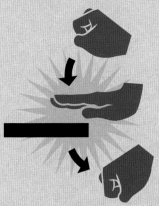

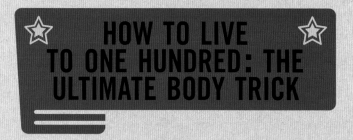

HOW TO LIVE TO ONE HUNDRED: THE ULTIMATE BODY TRICK

Most people would like to live longer, maybe even forever. For the moment though, let's shoot for an age that many people have hit but most sadly won't: one hundred years old.

There's no quick fix for longevity. If there was, we'd all live well into our second century. Here, however, are some tips for improving your odds of making it into the Century Club.

1. Keep active. A sedentary lifestyle can lead to obesity, heart troubles, and many more troubles. Regular exercise staves off risk factors for many types of diseases.

2. Have good genes. You have no control over this, of course, but the longer your parents and grandparents live, the better your chances of beating their records.

3. Avoid alcohol, caffeine, and tobacco. These can damage or put stress on your body in all sorts of ways.

4. Get regular check-ups. Seeing your doctor every year or more helps make sure you catch any problems early.

ABOUT THE AUTHOR

Michael Powell has always been interested in doing things he shouldn't. His hobbies include looking gift horses in the mouth, staring directly at solar eclipses, and blowing past speed traps up and down Route 66. An accomplished humor author with more than sixty titles under his belt, he lives a surprisingly relaxed life at home in England with his wife and two young children.